Becaus

Written by:
Jacky L. Robinson Jr.

Cadmus Publishing
www.cadmuspublishing.com

Published by Cadmus Publishing
www.cadmuspublishing.com
Port Angeles, WA

ISBN: 978-1-63751-146-6
Library of Congress Control Number: 2021925795

Book Cover Art: Dennis Hazard #357440
Typing by: Jane Eichwald at Ambler Document Processing

If you would like to donate in support of my bookpublishing please go online to one of the following sites. By doing so, you are helping me invest in God's Kingdom as well as investing in yourself! Thank you for your support. Go To: J-Pay.com or WesternUnion.com Jacky L. Robinson Jr #419058

Cheshire Correctional Institution 900 Highland Ave. Cheshire, Connecticut 06410

Dedication

To you, the reader.

A PERSONAL WORD

To all those I've misled throughout my time in the Ohio Prison system, my sincerest apologies. To those who became my brothers or close associates—violence is not nor will ever be the answer. We must grow in spiritual wisdom and learn to use our power and influence to help save lives, not destroy them. Sean $, Black James, Fathead, you all have a higher purpose. It's not an ordinary one and discovering it will not be easy, but nothing has ever been easy for men like us. The Kingdom of God needs you ...it awaits you. I love you.

George, Patty, William, Jacky Sr., Novella, thank you for not giving up on me and for loving me and supporting me all these years. I love you.

Tammy, thank you for having a forgiving spirit and for loving me through all the growing pains.

Cynthia D, thank you for helping me understand myself and for disciplining me as hard as you did while in S.O.C.F. The pressure you applied has brought forth a diamond! Your strength and charm is amazing.

Lebron James, we need you for governor in Ohio!!!

*   *   *

God wants us to learn how to embrace each and every part of our journey. The good and bad parts. The parts that make sense to us and the parts that are overwhelmingly confusing. Because God is never confused when we are or at any stage. He's never afraid. He's never out of control or unaware of us. Our actions may take us by surprise at times, but we will never surprise God. He's all-knowing. There will be times when you feel you're off track or out of alignment with God's will. But as long as you persist in prayer, asking God's will to be done at each step, He will amaze you when you finally reach a place where you can look back and see how He guided you and worked everything out for your good. This is what prayer is all about: a relationship with our Father and Creator. He takes good care of us and our needs and we take care of what He needs. God's purposes will always be completed, but He wants us to willingly accept and participate in accomplishing His plans—our willingness shows love and honor to Him. This is the "death to self" or "dying daily" that Scripture instructs us on. Christ teaches that we must die to selfish motives and intentions and pick up our cross and follow him if we really desire the new and abundant life he came to give us. God's blessings are released in our lives through obedience. His power and presence is released through our obedience. We obey because we love Him. And we love Him because He first loved us.

*   *   *

Ever since I was a child, I possessed a warrior's spirit. Though often told I would amount to nothing, I sought to surpass all things.

No one believed or gave me directions on what road to take, so I learned to listen to the whispers of the wind as they guided me along secret pathways that twisted and turned, bruised and burned the depth of my being.

This is unique, I noticed.
Unique to me in ways that speak to only I inside, the life inside yearning to be free.

I traveled. Pursuing a peace, I had yet to understand had always been within me.

A foreigner in both space and time, I found no rest. External forces unrelenting as the pressures mounted. Wanting to escape the reality of such confusion.

I sat my journey aside for another soul to pick up, It became too much...too weak to reach, too distant to touch.

"You must not give up."

I had to recall the lessons I learned. Where I am is not where I want to be.

Lesson one: Each journey unique. Lesson two: Know your worth.

Lesson three: Speak and believe. Lesson four: Persist in all things.

At that moment I knew I had reached the highest level of elevation. Vividly conscious of heightened senses, I extended my arm, taking hold of what was rightfully mine. The freedom to be me.

—Me

*   *   *

Intelligent, well-spoken, charismatic, generous, strong, funny, thoughtful, nice...All qualities within me that people have complimented by pointing out mostly in my late twenties and on. But these qualities didn't manifest overnight. It took some painful experiences to morph into the man I am today. I'm still growing. But thank God I'm not any of the negative or horrific labels that family and childhood friends stamped me with early on in life. Not in my heart where it matters. But for years I had given into these opinions and ideas from others in sad attempts to please them. Other times it was about survival and other times I had tried convincing myself that I was the bad guy people said I was due to being so confused and exhausted trying to discover more of my identity. At this confused stage I had no awareness of how a son can be visited by the sins of his father or even forefathers.

Just like a newborn baby can carry on a virus or physical ailment passed down from a parent, so too the spiritual ailments were transferable. I hadn't been taught these lessons in school, at home, by friends or in the streets where I grew up. I learned this the most difficult ways possible. Experiences. Not everyone learns from their pain, however. But as for me, I saw a dire need in responding to these innumerable events of abnormalities, choosing to open myself up to examine and study why these overwhelming feelings and experiences existed within and around me. I chose to look inside myself with the help of one true friend.

Contents

CHAPTER 1

I was introduced to the Islamic faith at the age of ten or so. My aunt and uncle would take me, my cousins and sisters to the Mosque on Howard Street on the north side of Akron, Ohio. The teachings in the Mosque were so different from what I had been taught in the Baptist church growing up. In hindsight it was like God was showing me the two covenants taught in the bible—Hagar and Sarah.

The nation of Islam even taught us karate as kids. The principles of self- discipline, unity, family and love was definitely something that was completely absent from my upbringing and much needed. However, my aunt and uncle never modeled or carried on those lessons in their household. In fact, it was the total opposite in all the houses I would temporarily reside in. Physical and sexual abuse, violence and extreme dysfunction was the norm.

My biological mother had given up me and my two older sisters when I was born.

My grandmother ended up taking custody for us when I was around two. Her household was filled with chaos and screams from the violence she inflicted on us. I learned to make her alcoholic beverages by the time I was seven.

"Seagram's extra dry gin in a glass with a slice of lemon and one cold Bush beer." This was her daily concoction after work.

It didn't take long for me to start running away as I got older. The fear of her eventually killing me with a frying pan to the head was motivation in my feet to run and run fast. At some point within my first several years living with her, she had allowed other family members to move in with us on 995 Avon Street. A three-bedroom house, sometimes holding seven to nine members was suffocating to say the least. My grandmother had given birth to nine children including my mother so there never was a shortage of family members in need of a "temporary" place to sleep. My aunts and uncles all bore children—some had three to five. And guess where they would sleep during their visit? Yup. Right in the area I was given—the basement.

The police and Children Services Board (C.S.B.) were regular visitors to the house that kept the secrets. It was odd because no matter how much my sisters and cousins would suffer abuse in that house, I was the only one who would muster up enough courage to actually tell the police whenever they'd take us away. The bruises, scars and open wounds were evidence enough for them I'm sure, but man did I feel alone explaining to the social workers how afraid I felt returning there.

The eighties crack epidemic really hit home. Most of my family, including my mom and dad, fell victim to the drug. So, by the time I was born in 1984, my dad maybe had a few moments with me before drugs re-directed his life. He lived a life of high and crime which landed him six prison numbers and on mental health medications before I turned eighteen. I would try to find love and comfort in the rough streets of Akron, Ohio. Avon Street was a nice working-class neighborhood, but several streets over was where I first began selling the same drug that helped destroy my family. Crack cocaine.

*   *   *

Before my first drug transaction, I'd steal out of stores or people's homes to eat and would even break in cars to sleep or sneak on random porches at night. The winter season was brutal at these times, but living on the streets was far better than living in that house with people who were supposed to be family. Since I was so young, whenever I'd run away from my grandmother's residence and the police found me, they'd either take me back to C.S.B. or to an aunt or uncle's house. And since my aunts and uncles were comfortable with passing down the same illegal ways of treatment on us children, it was never too long before I'd end up right back in the streets, sleeping in cars, on porches and in parks.

My sisters thought I was crazy, but I thought they were crazy for choosing to remain victims of abuse. It was too much for me, and without even knowing how, at those ages I knew it was wrong.

My grandad ended up drinking himself to death. My grandmother had emasculated him so much in front of us by beating him and cursing his every move that I was surprised he never committed suicide. He would sometimes hit me whenever I refused to listen, but for the most part he was also a victim.

At twelve me and two friends attempted to break into a car to steal the items inside, but instead were caught by authorities and charged with our very first juvenile crime. My criminal history worsened from there.

I didn't have many friends growing up. No birthday parties or cakes. No video games as a child and very few toys. Not much of an imagination as a boy either, other than imagining how different my life might have been if my mom loved me enough to return for me. This I thought about a lot. I mean—I yearned for the presence of my dad intensely, but that aching in my heart for my mother is what I recall most.

She'd call my grandmother's house once a year or so to speak to me and my sisters, and I would always break down in tears, begging her to come rescue me. At that tender age I didn't understand why she'd say things like, "I can't right now." I'd innocently think to myself, *The same way you dropped us off in a car you can come pick us up.* The pain and agony in her voice over the phone hurt me all the more. It was like her and I were connected to the depth of our emotions.

The last time I saw my mother was when I was fifteen, right before being sentenced to a year in the Department of Youth Services (D.Y.S.)

for multiple home burglaries. I served a total of two years and three months due to repeated acts of violence that continued adding months to my sentence.

At fifteen my mother had visited us from Florida where she had moved. She was off crack by now to my knowledge, but greatly enjoyed smoking marijuana. Her visit was brief—a couple days—before a family conflict broke out due to years of unresolved issues leading to her dramatic departure. I again was at a loss for words. But not tears.

D.Y.S. was just like the streets of Akron I ran in except the juveniles were from various cities and gangs. They were rowdy, violent, unfriendly and unpredictable. My life story. One would think I'd fit into this lifestyle, but no, I didn't. Neither did I want to. All I ever really wanted was a place to call home. To love and to be loved. To be accepted and to grow.

D.Y.S. posed a serious threat to my sanity because unlike the streets where I could walk or run from a problem too big, there was no escaping these interactions. Did I mention I was on the track team in middle school? Well, that was a skill I had become good at in the streets whenever neighborhood gangs and bullies came for me. It did me absolutely no good where I found myself now. I was forced to learn how not only to protect myself, but also to be the aggressor when necessary. I knew how to throw punches and kicks from my early exposure at the Mosque, watching grandma and family scuffles and personal neighborhood tussles, but these juveniles were being knocked unconscious by each other and attacked at levels of speed and power that made me question my capabilities. It was wild! Nevertheless, I felt my life on the line if I didn't adapt quickly. So after introducing myself to the Bloods, I was placed in E-Echo, the gang unit at Indian River, and slowly began to conform to more intense ways of violence.

I would oftentimes have to force myself to use violence because my heart was so far out of touch with this reality. I felt myself being pulled in two opposite directions all the time.

Witnessing non-violent juveniles being tortured was a wake-up call for me to conclude that I could not fall into the victim category. I quickly learned the influence, power and control I could possess through violent outbursts, which eventually helped me reach the top of the food chain as an adult later on in the Ohio prison system. The sins of my Father were visiting me.

CHAPTER 2

Directly next door to 995 Avon was a church, North Hill Baptist, owned by Pastor Hosea. Directly across the street from 995 was 996 where a white family lived. When I first began running away from home I'd only go as far as the house across the street.

The man and woman had a son, William, who was a few years older than me. The three of them lived in a two-bedroom house where William had his very own room. Whenever I'd scramble over in fear, banging on their door, they would lovingly step out of the way, allowing me safe passage inside. I'd search for a place to hide. All three of them would lay hands on me, praying out loud in the name of Jesus Christ, asking God to protect me. After praying they'd let me stay a little while longer as they spoke amongst themselves deciding what exactly to do next. I'd beg them not to call the police, because every time the police spoke to my grandmother it would only ignite her more and I'd suffer once they'd leave. With very few options, they'd settle on walking me back over to that house, asking my grandmother things such as, "Is everything all right? Can Jacky stay the night with us?" Of course, she'd pretend things were okay, refusing to let them keep me, but the screams from that house never fooled any of our neighbors. (They shared this with me when I became an adult.)

I really didn't know what was worse when it came to my grandmother—the police or the "white man." She was a huge southern woman who hated both and wasn't afraid to express so to us children whenever they weren't around. 996 Avon was the first white family out of two who, as I looked back, I was able to see the hand of God work through. Both white families were deeply rooted Christians. Their households were full of love, peace, discipline, and unity. These being the same principles or "fruits" that so many different religions teach, but the full manifestation of them being evident within these families.

I couldn't understand why my family was so different, so evil in contrast, or why was I the only one in my family being drawn to this "other life."

*   *   *

I didn't grasp many positive experiences from juvenile hall or the youth centers. And the few deeply ingrained events that did assist with my maturity, I recall well. One is of a male staff member in juvenile hall. Mr. Jennings. He was a muscle-bound black man who enjoyed sharing his wisdom with us juvies. It was more of the elegance he spoke with that affected me most. To be so big and strong he was a very gentle speaking man, even with the deep bass.

I remember being fourteen in Dan Street, Juvenile Hall. I was arrested for a probation violation. At this point in my life I was recklessly involved in sexual activities with many girls without protection. I was romantically connected with one particular female who I would stay with on and off, but the thrill of the streets would not let me settle down completely.

Sitting in a plastic chair in the dayroom one early morning, I noticed how irritated and itchy my pubic hairs had been. I kept disregarding it after scratching for a moment or two seemed to relieve my discomfort, but then the irritation would return soon after. This went on for nearly an hour before I decided to reach inside my jumpsuit to feel around.

What's the problem, I thought. I knew very little about sexually transmitted diseases. I was smart and a fast learner in school, but with all the drama with my house placements, I couldn't focus much on books, so I acted out a lot which resulted in me being placed into a severe behavior program during school hours. So, if one of my teachers did teach on the subject of "crabs," I had completely missed the curriculum. No need to tell you how terrified, confused and physically ill I became when I yanked a tiny bug from between my hairs, examining it closely.

What in the world?!

I was so creeped out by the sight that I could feel chills all over my body as sweat beaded up on my forehead. I tossed it to the floor in pure ignorance, thinking my problem had been solved, no more itchy-ness. But it continued. Bug after bug.

Yank. Discard. Sweat. I didn't understand.

This went on for hours before I finally asked Mr. Jennings to speak with him in private. I was so embarrassed.

"I need to tell you something," I mumbled.

His focus intent. I wasn't the type to complain about just anything. He knew it had to be a serious issue. I spoke at a whisper. "I don't know what's going on, but I keep pulling these little bugs off my pubic hairs and they keep coming back."

I lifted one up to his face to show him. This six-foot thick-bearded man jumped back, snatching my bony wrist with his hand so fast I thought he'd slam me to the floor. My eyes widened with fear.

It's only a bug, right, I thought to myself. "Boy! Not so close," he huffed.

He lowered my hand by the wrist, hunching over to take a look, my fingertips opening to reveal the puny creature.

"Uugggh." He looked disgusted. I had to be the reddest black boy by now. "It's okay. I'll get you fixed up."

He knew just what to do. He exited the block after ordering me to undress in the shower. Mr. Jennings returned with a large bottle of clear liquid and a small black metal-like comb. I applied the shampoo from head to toe in all my hairy areas, letting its oak in for the length of time he had directed. Then, with the comb I stepped into the shower water and guided it through all the areas as I rinsed off. Meanwhile, all the other juveniles sat calmly in the dayroom, watching videos on TV. None paying any attention to this life-altering moment I was in.

At no time did Mr. Jennings make a scene about me being "infected" or purposely cause me more discomfort, even though staff were known for getting their jokes off on juvies who had unpleasant situations such as peeing in bed, snoring, etc. This man kept cool the whole way through. Afterwards, the nurse handed me some pamphlets with very detailed information about S.T.D.s, how to use condoms, the works! I soaked up the information and downloaded it into my memory chip like my destiny depended on it, because it did. I felt so much better that night as I closed my eyes in the bunk to sleep. But shortly after relaxing, my mind once again began to race. I didn't have time to rest. I had to figure out where my life was headed. A decision that no fourteen-year-old should ever have to make on his own.

* * *

I didn't know God or Jesus Christ at these stages in my life. Allah, Buddha, Jehovah ...none of these names or titles held any personal meaning to me. I didn't have a mommy or daddy. My two older sisters were somewhere. Only God knew. No tone friend who could genuinely relate or cared enough to relate to my pain.

Even speaking with social workers and mental health professionals as I grew older, not one of them ever said, "I understand what you're going through. I want to help you." Would these words have made a difference? I don't know. Maybe. Maybe not, but it would've at least been comforting to hear them at one of these times in my life. Perhaps they would've left an impression big enough for me to recall now. But no, not one memory of them. There had always been a wide disconnect when sharing my battles with others. Needless to say, unable to cope with these inner struggles I turned out to be on some serious psychological medications by the time I was sixteen. Doctors had diagnosed me with severe depression, anxiety and a list of other things.

By the time I was released from D.Y.S. at eighteen, my dad had purchased a nice two-bedroom house for me to live in with him and my stepmother. He'd finally broken his addiction to crack cocaine and was mentally stable enough with medications to receive custody of me through juvenile parole authorities.

The first time I lived with my dad right before I was sent to D.Y.S., things didn't work out well. I was fifteen and felt independent enough to make my own choices in life, often rebelling against him which caused tensions and climaxed to me stealing his car and going missing. So now at eighteen with the crazy wild lifestyle I'd undergone in D.Y.S. for over two years, I was willing to accept his help, seeing his hand as an attempt to rectify the wrongs in our past, but taking any orders was beyond imaginable. I'd outgrown being mistreated by family or anyone. And although my dad never physically hit or abused me (with the exception of pushing me once at fifteen), my mindset towards life in a whole was to strike at anyone who posed a threat to my emotions or space. My character was gradually taking the form of those who had initially controlled my life. And no matter how loud my heart screamed out, *you are not this person!!*, the course was set.

This defiant and hostile attitude showed itself little by little over the period of thirty days living with them. I struggled finding a job and got tired living off them. I started to realize that if I wanted a better lifestyle, I had to return to what I knew best. The streets. Since my street connections were still present and available due to the energies I was putting out into the universe, it was easy for me to locate drugs, guns and whatever else I wanted to engage in. My mentality became far more dangerous in this bully-state, because I didn't respond well to other so-called bullies. Then whenever I encountered childhood bullies, I felt it necessary to retaliate in some manner or another for the damage they'd done to me in such innocent years. I was walking in the dark alleys of un-forgiveness. And it was because of this that I wasn't able to see or accept what great opportunities that were presented to me by others. Some by complete strangers.

What I'm saying is that at eighteen I'd been shown ways to alter the destructive path my life had taken. The legitimate money, resources and people came knocking.

But because my spirit was so unclean, holding on to bitterness, anger and pride, I settled for far less than I was truly worth. And what was so sad was that I didn't recognize my worth, but others did. It wasn't until many, many years after being in prison that my eyes were opened and I began to see in me what others had seen all along. I just thank God it wasn't too late.

*   *   *

After roughly four months as a free man, I was back in confinement, but this time I was introduced to adult jail, not juvenile. The saying, "old places, old faces, new cases" proved true. Smoking marijuana, drinking alcohol, selling drugs and carrying guns led me to two charges of aggravated murder. I didn't calm down much, even after my arrest, picking fights with others in the county jail. I was bitter, filled with rage and in search of something or someone I knew nothing about.

I immediately noticed the Ohio prison system was a strangely conducted zoo.

Man, had I wished I'd turned my life around far before now. It was unbelievable! The violence level was insane. Stabbings, people being attacked with locks in a sock, inmates being thrown off the top tiers, guards being beaten down, street drugs, chaos, more drugs, inmates being raped in showers and cells, gang-bangin', female guard prostitution, P.D.A. (Prisoner Displays of Affection), feces fights, inmate suicides, staff bullies, riots ...It got so bad by my second year in prison that I tried to overdose by swallowing a handful of psychotropic medications. I laid down on the bunk shortly after, expecting my heart to stop at some point. The beating continued.

Over the period of three years or so my attempts at suicide had tripled, but to no avail. I would be hospitalized in a mental health unit or in Oakwood psychiatric ward, but never successful with ending my life like countless other inmates had been. One of my close friends from Cleveland, Ohio, Marques, had accomplished his suicidal mission at the age of twenty-four. So why couldn't I? My frustration and fears only intensified as I grew more and more violent, assaulting officers, engaging in riots, stabbing inmates. It became a survival game ironically. The prison elements were so unpredictable that it often felt like 995 Avon all over. I couldn't live like this. I needed control.

Since my inclusion into the Bloods gang at Indian River, I had become a student of their history. Most of my studies would take place in isolation or segregation where I spent a lot of time as a juvenile and adult, because of violent incidents. Prison gangs were more structured than juvenile. This afforded me opportunities to absorb knowledge of the movements and roots of every faction. I sought to climb the ladder of ranks, seeing how the leaders of each group moved with confidence and security. They were untouchable to opposing gangs, because they possessed power and influence over their sets. They could start a huge riot with one word. Inmates both feared and respected this. So did the guards and warden. I needed this control over my life. This was what I lacked.

I began studying books such as George Jackson, Huey P. Newton, Bobby Seal, Tookie Williams, Malcolm X, and Marcus Garvey, to gain insight into both black history and gang history and quickly learned how black and black violence had not been the original intent. The base laws within gangs were the same as the religions I had learned about: the need for family, unity, love, respect.

"Wow!" I marveled. The lack of family support and love in-home had pushed me into the homes of total strangers as a child—now this. This was interesting.

Books such as Huey P. Newton's *Revolutionary Suicide* held special meaning to me. I was witnessing and experiencing so much oppression and corruption from staff in prisons I'd be sent to that I had no other choice than to spiritually bond with the struggle. I climbed in power through knowledge and violence, helping to enlighten the minds of all those who were also seeking to understand and find purpose to their lives. It was as if the very spirits of Malcolm and Sylvester had visited me, filling me with their pain and desire for revenge they had died with. I played host, becoming the voice of the people—my people. Those oppressed. Blind. Broken. Abused. Corrupted. Silenced.

Alive and dead. I became a leader.

This entire time throughout my growth and development stages as an aspiring Blood leader, prison officials were powerless to stop me from reaching fullness. Not that they were afraid to hang me up in a cell and call my family, stating I had committed suicide (This was spoken of happening often to the most hated inmates.). Instead, it was the calling on my life that actually prevented them from taking it this far. Not the gang-life, but what God had planned for my life far before my conception.

In the winter of 2011, I initiated a gang-riot between the Bloods and a fast-paced up and coming street gang/prison gang known as the Heartless Felons. This riot lasted for several weeks in Southern Ohio Correctional Facility, also known as Lucasville. Each time the prison would be let off lockdown, violence would ensue. This particular prison was known for great disturbances and staff racism. The staff population at the time was 95% white and only added more tension to the division already apparent within the many gangs.

Only a few days had passed from the first inmate on inmate gang altercation before we turned our rage against staff. I was placed in 4-B segregation for a total of sixteen months.

I never got used to being in segregation. It was always uncomfortable and abnormal to me, especially with the extremely long lengths of time I would be sentenced to spend: eighteen months, sixteen months, five months, twelve months, seven months.

However, I adapted my mind and body to the setting in order to keep what little sanity I had left. I was older now with actual suicide attempts behind me, but never completely dismissing the idea. Times were hard. The few family members who were by my side during all this, couldn't understand why I stayed in trouble. I endeavored explaining as best I could, most times being open and honest to the point of gruesome details of an attack I had done or that was done to me. I'd receive letters back from my family plainly stated: "I don't know what to say," furnishing evidence of the shock value on their minds. I wasn't expecting them to say much anyway. I mean, what could anyone say at this point that would be helpful? I was turning into someone even I didn't like, but felt necessary to let live. I used to run from violence at 995 and in the streets of Akron. Now I was literally running it; placing hit orders on both inmates and staff.

At some point throughout all of this I was lured to spiritual awakening books and literature on the invisible realms around me. I was drawn into studying numerology and astrology in search of the significance behind my birthdate and the number nineteen I kept seeing all around me. It was as if this number was inviting me to claim it. But for what I wasn't sure. All I knew was that every time I'd see it pop up, I'd get excited and mesmerized by its inherent powers over me. I hadn't known that numbers were spiritual or how people obsessively used them as guides in life. So whenever possible I applied myself to search for the truth.

One of the beautiful things about God is that He interacts with us on whatever level we are on mentally and spiritually. What He shows me today would've frightened me to death ten years ago or been far below my level of consciousness. He elevated me at each stage in my life as I sought to discipline myself to learn. But the bulk of my attention went first and foremost to surviving the conditions of prison life.

Being one of the most notorious gang leaders in the system proved immensely beneficial, but also came with some serious stress. By the time I was twenty-eight, prisons were filling up with more and more eighteen and nineteen-year-olds with life sentences unlike when I was incarcerated. Back then the eighteen-year-olds with long sentences were spread out to various prisons. Now they were being collected in crowds and transferred wherever there was space. They were loud, disrespectful, and eager to earn whatever stripes they could. I commenced recruiting these youngins; bestowing guidance, extending protection, and family unity. Each and every morning when I'd awake, I was no longer thinking only of myself, but I now had to think and move for the well-being and success of my team.

Reputation and name meant everything. Prison Administration and officials acknowledging me as a threat, turning heads at my brazen illegal drug deals and hit orders. The power and respect was real. I demanded it. I had earned it. After fourteen years of climbing up this mountain, I soon became winded, feeling drained of my life force, knowing that my full potential was not manifested in this life. I didn't know what to do or where to turn. I was exhausted from being someone else, entertaining the spirits of those who had already lived their life. *Had I thought this would last forever?* It wasn't truth. And I soon began to discover that I had been wired to abide in truth.

Me.

Jacky Robinson, Jr.

My life.

Created.

Given.

For truth.

My present circumstances would not just allow me to wave goodbye to a lie I had shed blood to build. I knew that much. Though I had to do something. There was a secret life I had been feeding while in segregation areas. One where I had developed writing abilities; penning a total of four books and where I had designed several legitimate businesses, even going as far as starting one with the help of my dad and stepmom. Segregation helped bring out a side of me I wasn't aware existed …A side of me I had to keep hidden from the prison population, because I knew I could be killed with my head in the clouds chasing a dream. In seg' I dared to dream. Now these dreams wanted to live through me!?

How could they be so selfish?!! Oscar Wilde wrote:

> "The vilest deeds, like poison weeds bloom well within prison air. It is only what is good inside man that withers and dies there."

The relentless urge to become something more kicked my creative energies into overdrive. If I wanted to be some sort of positive creator or whatever this other life was calling me to be, then I'd first need to remove myself from this crippling prison environment, I finally concluded. And since I knew I wasn't innocent of the crimes, I decided I'd have to give birth to one last lie. But this was it, I promised the energies around me.

CHAPTER 3

When God said, "let's make man in our image," He truly did just that. People get so absorbed with the physical appearance that they fail to realize what's beneath the exterior. God wasn't speaking about the outer appearance. God is spirit. Our spirit is our life force, the part that possesses the image of God. The part that cannot be destroyed. The part that gives us meaning and purpose. Our innate ability to create and destroy is an attribute of God. God is a Creator and also a destroyer. In Scripture, He destroyed towns and people for unrepentant evil ways and He created life to bring forth beauty, love and more life to all of His Creation. Both man and woman do the exact same today by applying this divine ability to either create or destroy. The intent, of course, is immensely different from God's most of the time, but the ability continues on. We produce after our own kind.

On September 30, 2014 I knowingly, willingly and manipulatively used my God-given ability to have my case reopened in the Akron, Ohio Summit County Courthouse. This was how it went:

In 2012 I'd met an inmate by the name of Demian Duncan while

I was in segregation in S.O.C.F. This meeting occurred a few weeks after the gang riot between Bloods and Heartless Felons. This inmate had expressed his admiration of me upon hearing stories from other inmates about who I had become while in prison. He too was from Akron, Ohio and close to my age, so we began to build a friendship that neither of us imagined would put our names in newspapers, Facebook, and in newsletters.

After a few months of an evolving friendship with this guy, I began to entertain the idea of paying him to become a false witness for me in order to get me released. I carefully wrote out the details on paper and lowered it down to his cell on the bottom tier, using a sock attached to a prison-made clothesline.

"Read this and get back with me," I wrote on the outside of the letter. It only took a few moments.

"I got you, whatever you need!"

I was pleasantly surprised at his enthusiasm to assist me with concocting such a bold lie. My creative forces dug deeper. The next letter I wrote him hours later was a longshot I knew. No one in their right mind would be willing to do such a thing. The power and influence I had in the prison system in addition to being a risk-taker, boosted my confidence. I wrote: "Bro, after thinking about it, you being a witness for me won't really help much. Since I pleaded guilty to the crimes, the courts won't be willing to re- open my case off that alone. We need to come up with a more solid game plan to get me home…

Here's where things got serious. This man only had roughly ten years left before his release date. I was about to ask him to do something that could very well keep him in prison for the rest of his life!

"This is what I came up with. If you write an affidavit saying that you were the one who actually committed the crimes I'm in prison for and explain in detail about the crime scenes, the courts will have no other choice than to free me! Think about it, you were home when I committed these crimes, so it's not like they can say you are lying.

Only you and me will know the truth! You won't get any extra time because I'll have my family and friends protest for us both and pay for good lawyers who will argue against punishing you for doing the 'right thing'—coming forward. It's perfect! Plus, I'll pay you for helping me."

I sat on the bunk in my small cell, feeling a whirlwind of emotions. I was excited at the possibilities if he responded with a yes, but also extremely nervous if his reply was no. If no, then I would have to decide the path of our relationship. I would probably have to treat him as an enemy. He knew entirely too much of my vision for freedom and the Malcolm X "Any Means Necessary" mentality I had to achieve it. I could sense his heart was good. He genuinely desired to help a fellow prisoner of war, but how far would he be willing to go to aid the mission? My anxiety got the best of me before he responded. I enclosed another scribe inside the sock, swinging it down to him.

"I didn't have any co-defendants on my cases and you don't have to worry about naming anyone else as a witness or accomplice. We're not snitching on anyone. The entire point is to get me home so I can put this life behind me, bro. I'm fed up with this prison nonsense. I need another chance at freedom.

P.S. Send me these notes back when you're done reading them so I can flush them. Not that I don't trust you. My toilet works better.

"K.I."

K.I. was an acronym for the nickname Killa Instinct given to me by an associate of mine named Goldie who was from Cleveland, Ohio. He, after witnessing how fierce I was when attacking opponents, told me that I possessed a Killer Instinct. The name stuck.

Five minutes passed.

Silence.

I paced the cell plotting five chess moves ahead on what ifs.

"Bro, shoot the line down to me!" he yelled out from the cell bars.

I took my time lowering the line as to not appear affected either way by his answer. Inwardly, however, the little child was far from settle down. So much at stake.I opened the note.

"Look, I don't know much about law, but it sounds like you do. I want to help you in any way I can, but you are going to have to tell me step by step what to say and what to do. My life is in your hands. If you say I won't get more time then good, because I wanna go home after my sentence is up. I don't have any family or money so whatever you pay me for this will be appreciated. I got you...I'll do it", Demian.

That was all I needed. A willing participant. I nearly cried I was so happy. This gave me hope. I knew there was a real possibility of him taking my life sentences, but I promised to do whatever necessary to prevent that from happening, and I always tried to be a man of my word.

The next step was getting some money on his commissary account so he could see my loyalty. I wrote a letter to the streets handling that. I then took him under my wing for protection. I provided him a list of names of guys in prisons throughout Ohio—Bossmen, shot callers who would provide for and protect him on the strength of me. He was officially off limits to any past or present enemy he had. I wrote other head Blood members informing them of the new family recruit. The Bloods and Crips outnumbered every other gang in the system until the Heartless Felons took root. However, a bunch of H-F's were either former or aspiring Blood members.

On September 30, 2014, months after I was transferred from S.O.C.F. level four maximum prison to Toledo level three and four prison (this being my second transfer to this institution), my lawyer, Jana Deloach, filed a motion within the Summit County Courts to withdraw my two guilty pleas based on Newly Discovered Evidence. That evidence being Demian Duncan's three-page notarized affidavit confessing sole responsibility for the crimes I had been convicted of. I convinced my lawyer of cop corruption, claiming my guilty pleas were coerced by detectives. She believed me. I had my family professionally design t-shirts: *Exonerate Jacky*

I began planning organized protests in front of the courthouse to gain publicity on my innocence; only me and Demian knowing the truth of what was really happening. I felt so terrible lying to my family and fiancé about the entire situation, but I convinced myself that it was all for a good cause. I needed to get home to build a new life and do something positively constructive with the many talents I'd unearthed from within me.

I was denied a hearing on the new evidence at the county level as was somewhat expected. After filing in the Ohio Ninth District Court of Appeals the ruling was strongly in my favor:

Man who pleaded guilty to murder wins appeal; case heads back to court

ANNIE YAMSON
Special to the Legal News
Published: November 9, 2015

The 9th District Court of Appeals recently ordered a trial court to look at all of the evidence in a murder case before denying an inmate's motion to withdraw his guilty plea.

The district court's review of the case stemmed from Jacky Robinson Jr.'s 2005 conviction in the Summit County Court of Common Pleas on charges of aggravated murder and aggravated burglary with firearm specifications. The victim in the case was Dennis Ober.

Before that conviction, Robinson had pleaded guilty to the murder of Grover Jones in a separate case and he was serving that prison sentence when he was implicated in Ober's murder and questioned by police.

Ultimately, Robinson also pleaded guilty to Ober's murder and was sentenced to life imprisonment.

According to court documents, on Sept. 30, 2014, Robinson filed a motion to withdraw his guilty pleas and he attached a letter written by a man named Demian Duncan.

The letter was addressed to Robinson's father and, in it, Duncan admitted to committing both murders.

Also attached to the motion were affidavits from Duncan and Robinson.

Duncan apparently wrote the letter from the Southern Ohio Correctional Facility, where he is currently serving a 16-year sentence on multiple robbery convictions and where Robinson was also incarcerated at the beginning of his prison term.

In his affidavit, Robinson claimed that he only confessed to murdering Jones after police officers told him that his girlfriend, Dusty Woods, was suffering an asthma attack in a nearby cell.

He alleged that the officers threatened to keep her there until he confessed.

Robinson stated that he only gave his confession after he received a call from Woods, who told him that she was being questioned by police and was possibly going to be charged.

He maintained that both of his confessions were false and that he made them to help Woods.

Robinson also attested that he "did not know until years later the true events that happened with Jones, Ober and Duncan."

The Summit County court denied the motion without a hearing, stating in its judgment entry that "the only purported evidence attached in support of Robinson's motion is what appears to be a confession letter from Duncan."

"The court gives no weight to this letter," the judgment entry states. "Robinson has not provided the court with any other evidentiary materials in support of his claims."

The trial court concluded that Robinson failed to meet his burden on establishing the existence of a manifest injustice that would warrant a withdrawal of the pleas and that his claim was barred by res judicata."

The court of appeals disagreed.

"In his sole assignment of error, Robinson contends that the trial court erred by denying his motion to withdraw his guilty plea," Judge Julie Schafer wrote on behalf of the court of appeals. "Specifically, he argues that the trial court failed to properly consider Duncan's affidavit that was attached to the original motion to withdraw and Robinson's affidavit that was attached to his reply brief."

Robinson also contended that his motion was not barred by res judicata.

"We agree on both points," Schafer wrote. "Here, three pieces of evidence were offered in support of Robinson's motion to withdraw his guilty plea."

Just as Robinson did, the appellate panel pointed at the letter and the two affidavits and noted that the trial court never addressed the affidavits, suggesting that it failed to consider them at all.

"In light of the trial court's failure to account for all of the evidentiary materials offered by Robinson, its decision to deny the motion to withdraw guilty pleas constituted an abuse of discretion," Schafer wrote.

The court of appeals declined to express any opinion on whether the trial court should hold a hearing on the matter.

Rather, it reversed the trial court's judgment with the sole instruction that it consider all of the evidence before ruling on the motion.

"Accordingly, we sustain Robinson's sole assignment of error," Schafer concluded.

Presiding Judge Beth Whitmore and Judge Carla Moore joined Schafer to form the majority.

The case is cited State v. Robinson, 2015-Ohio-4262.

[Back]

Talk about hope fulfilled! This was the manifestation of my dreams and ideas showing up for the world to see. I couldn't contain my joy. I shared the newspaper articles with everyone. A female officer called me a celebrity while opening up to me about how pretty her feet looked outside of her shoes. I basked in this new light of attention, no longer taking responsibility for the crimes I had committed on the truly innocent men. I was now the victim and at every turn I used it to my advantage.

My role as a gang leader took on a completely different style at this point.

Instead of being out in the open with my power, I sought to play behind the scenes roles from fear of anymore tragic events transpiring with my fingerprints all over it. I focused more intently on being a free man more than anything else. I had multiple women to choose from and mailed each of them a grocery list of items I would need upon my arrival home: Fruity Pebbles cereal, orange juice, grape juice, eggs, hamburger meat, pecan pie, marshmallows…

I felt rejuvenated. But it was only a matter of months before I would face another life-humbling experience. The same county court and judge who denied me the first time for a hearing, denied me a second time. To me it became personal. My family immediately paid another lawyer, named Jonathan Sinn, to climb on board with the second Appeal. My family's finances were dwindling. I had slowed down prison hustling to keep my hands clean, thinking my freedom was only weeks away. The idea of them financially providing more and more for me when I had become very capable of producing for them and myself was stressful. I wasn't sure how long this next Appeal would take or if the Appeals Court would even rule in my favor again. Even though Demian was still at S.O.C.F., I knew he'd still be in need of commissary and eventually that lawyer I promised, if we were granted the hearing.

Then there were the desperate faces of my team around me. The ones I had also come to know as family. They were looking to me to re-emerge at the front line to lead. The pressures mounted as I saw no other choice than to rise and live out my present reality. The alternative would be the extinction of everything I had built. I again took the ropes in hand, tightened my grip, and commanded courage as I created. The unseen positive forces at war with the negative forces all around and within me.

I chose a male correctional officer to engage in illegal business activities. We'd known each other for two years. He was from the streets of Toledo, Ohio and respected the way I carried myself in foreign territory. An incident had taken place between him and one of my older homies where it nearly got physical before I intervened. I swiftly extinguished the fire, earning well deserved points with him.

This officer had champagne wishes that his paycheck would not cover. I was in search of an outside connection who could package and deliver me the drugs and contraband I needed to make money and feed my team. We had a common interest. The trust was there. So, I broke down the mathematics to him; his percentage for muling, how to deliver, what to purchase in the streets, everything. His eyes were wide with anticipation as I divided the numbers. $800 a week for his cut and I'd profit $800 a week as well. I agreed to invest the initial $150. Three days later I received my first load. This wasn't the first time I'd engaged in illegal dealings or involvement with officers, but it was the first time with drugs in this volume. I was delivered ounces of marijuana at a time, along with Sub Oxone strips, K-2 and tobacco. I supplied the Mexicans, crips, felons, neutrals and Aryan Brotherhood with whatever they needed.

The money came in fast and steady: $500, $300, $250, $800. I opened up a joint bank account on the streets through a friend and built my credit. My team was eating and since I broke bread with the Heartless Felons and other gangs, there wasn't much tension or beef between anyone. I controlled my environment.

I was pumping so much drugs into the system that after a while I had to slow the flow, because everyone was supplied, which meant I would have to keep packages stashed for days or even a week and that was never safe for my holders. I could've pulled the cord at any time, ending my run. I had reached my financial goal, my family on the streets were ahead, I had lawyer money for Demian and my team in-house stacked enough money for commissary and lawyers. Everyone was set. But greed kicked in. It became a power high to me. *Why stop?* I questioned. My connect was fluffing his pillow at night with cash and he too became greedy. It wasn't long before he was pressured by inmates he'd known from the streets to bring in shipments for them. They jealously wheeled him in without my knowledge. Instead of being open and honest about it so I could have it handled, he kept it secret. Wrong move. That was all it took before the prison investigator and officers came raiding my cell and placing me in handcuffs at 1:00 a.m. I was transferred to two different prisons before Central Office decided to force me out of state. I was held in segregation at Ross Correctional Institution until another state agreed to accept me. The seven months in seg' dramatically changed my life. The events written next were mostly documented in real time at the time I experienced them.

CHAPTER 4

L ord. Savior ...I am with You."
The sudden appearance of the writing on the wall in the single cell I was in was clear. The words were from the Holy Bible as I blinked repeatedly to make certain I wasn't asleep or imagining them.

"...With You..."

I didn't understand what it meant. How are you "with me?" So many questions circled my mind. There wasn't anyone else in the cell around me.

An hour or so before, after falling asleep, I had heard a strong, but gentle voice as I awoke to turn over onto my other side. The voice spoke: "I will make you..." quoting Genesis 12:2-3, then said, "A thousand may fall ..." quoting Psalm 91. Now the appearance of these words as I awoke. The writing was alive and moving!

I lay on my right side facing the dirty brick wall in Cell 149, house 5-A. I was two months into my segregation bid awaiting the paperwork to be completed for my out-of-state transfer. The first month was one of my roughest seg' trips ever. Ross Correctional was one of the handful of institutions in Ohio that was infested with mice, roaches and huge spiders, none of which I'd grown used to despite being raised in houses overrun with them. Within my first thirty days I had killed at least a thousand different size roaches; some so long and fat I was afraid to smash! Even with the cell light on all day and night, these creatures were everywhere. I couldn't sleep, sit down or lay down for more than a few minutes before I was chasing them up and down the walls, bedframe, floor and ceiling. It was unbearable. Other inmates would scream out in terror throughout the day suffering the same battle. Even the food trays sometimes contained a live spider or roach. I examined each bite before eating.

At times I'd break down mentally, praying to God to deliver me. Other times thoughts of suicide popped into my head.

How long would I survive this, I wondered. There was the huge concern of how I'd manage in another state, being distant from family and friends. The fear of the unknown haunted me. Would I have to start re-building my reputation all over again from the bottom? I was getting too old for this. I'd just turned thirty-two, but my life experiences had really advanced my wisdom and demeanor. I was tired of this; at my breaking point once again with seemingly nowhere to turn. So, I picked up the bible.

I began searching for something...answers as to why I was going through this intense struggle in life. Was there any hope or way out? I needed peace. My mind was restless. I needed help. This wasn't the first time I studied Scripture. Mostly in isolation I'd seek comfort in God's word and would pray for His assistance with my life. It appeared He would never answer how I wanted Him to.

The moments of success I achieved in prison running a business or elevating in some manner, I credited to my own persistence and abilities or "universal energies." However, I wasn't completely out of touch with who Christ was or spiritual law. In 2005, I recall dropping to my knees in prayer and confession. But this was very different. Christ was actually speaking to me in ways I had only read about in the bible! Then came the dreams. I would see things, vivid images in my dreams at night. The next day or a week later the dream would play out in the daytime while I was walking to medical from seg' or going on a visit. I'd remember the dream in that instant and be filled with awe and wonder. I became fascinated with these supernatural encounters and started fasting and praying more throughout each week to understand.

Christ would speak to me through His Holy Spirit, leading me to particular Scripture verses he wanted me to learn. I became totally immersed in this spiritual world, expressing to my fiancé during monthly visits how incredibly alive I felt on the inside and how God would talk to me. She was shocked to say the least. She had no clue how to respond, often asking if I was losing my mind.

"If I haven't lost it by now after spending over eight years in seg," then I'm not losing it now," I told her.

I desperately needed her to know everything was okay and that her and I would be okay. All my assurance fell on deaf ears. This Jpay e-mail was from her:

JACKY ROBINSON JR A451317 RCI H5A149B ID:234872936 [P 1/3]

From: Tammy S Spraggins, CustomerID 3275058
To   JACKY ROBINSON JR ID A451317
Date : 9/20/2016 2:44:32 AM EST.   Letter ID: 234872936
Location RCI
Housing H5A149B
pre-paid stamp included

I received 3 emails from you this afternoon, and a 4th one this evening. Glad to know you're doing well. I will continue with the dissection method of responding if that is working for you starting with the email dated 9/15/16.

No, I changed my mind. I tried it, and it just didn't feel right, felt more like a tit for tat, so I have deleted my letter and am starting again. All I feel I can do at this point is apologize for not being more supportive initially, work to be more supportive in the future, and hope that you understand on some level where my response was stemming from.   But because I believe that your assessment isn't accurate, I'm going to at least attempt to correct that belief. We've talked before that changing one's belief is often futile, but I want to at least share my perspective, and you can take it or leave it.

You compared my response this time to my response when you first started studying numerology for the first time. This situation (or how I perceived it) was actually very similar to when you got those books. There were 2 major differences that impacted how I saw things and my ability to pull back and just be supportive back then versus how I initially responded now. One, when you first started studying numerology, we talked about other things as well, so it didn't feel like it was your ONLY focus. I mean, you shared your observations with me and included me.   The language that you used made me feel that numerology only confirmed and strengthened our bond. You also seemed to recognize that your zealousness was a bit overwhelming so you actively tried to temper it a bit. As you shared your raw experiences this time, I felt very much excluded, judged for where I was with spirituality which made me (right or wrong) defensive, and our relationship all of a sudden quite conditional on my acceptance of your position. It didn't feel good even though despite your perception to the contrary, I tried to find the positives if nothing else, for you (perhaps that didn't come through in my emails, though). Also, part of my conflicting feelings in this situation is wondering how to even tell someone...anyone, but especially you who was so excited and exuberant...that their spiritual change was coming so fast and so strong that it was actually concerning. I mean, how is it ever bad to "obsess" about God? And how do you say that without being offensive? Was it normal? Because I've rarely experienced the level you displayed. Was isolation getting to you somehow? Or was I just being some kind of sub-believing heathen?

Well, that wasn't the point I wanted to make with you I got off subject. Jacky, you said that "the level of fear of fear you live in and make decisions in threatens our relationship more than anything else. You've been thinking about and fearing this distance for so long now it's becoming a reality." You also said that I was operating out of things from "past seasons."
Jacky, my concerns about isolation changing or at least affecting our relationship are valid and very much about the here and now. They are not "fears" that have somehow manifested themselves. The reality is that separation does not in any way, shape or form promote intimacy. It detracts from it. Couples have to work very hard to stay close emotionally when they must be apart from each other, when they are not able to connect with each other (that is true, by the way, even when couples LIVE with each other but work or other obligations make their weeks busy .they have to recharge/reconnect in the evenings, on the weekends, etc to stay close).

In our situation, email as our primary form of communication has been less than helpful in keeping us close emotionally because of reactivity on both your and my parts (in my humble opinion), and we have become more distant with the conflict that that reactivity brings (I love you no less and I would hope the same is true of you, but our relationship has a different feeling to it which prompted my questions after our last visit). When you first when to seg, I kept trying to find ways to let you know I still needed you (which is really what I wanted from you so I thought if I modeled it, you would follow suit), but the more I expressed how much I was missing you, the more you seemed to see this as a negative. Perhaps because you wanted to "fix" how I was feeling, I don't know. But when you started focusing on your relationship with God, it felt more and more like you forgot about me (selfish I know). You once wrote about us needing to get back to us and our relationship but then your focus changed and you never came back to it. Over time, it felt like everything you wrote about was your case and God and changes to your life plan, when I also needed to know that we would still be good no matter what. Then your language shifted (as you know I pay attention to your words, just as you pay attention to mine). It was no longer about unconditional love and committed work on our relationship, about forever. Or you just wouldn't answer at all (which is very uncharacteristic of you so the omission was glaring). I did have a fear of losing you, but NOT because of the distance, but because of the reality of our communication gap and difficulty maintaining intimacy that this distance had caused and facilitates. You saw evidence of my sense of panic in my last couple of longer emails because it suddenly hit me that I couldn't control it. Like it hit me that I could really lose you because I couldn't change the distance, I seem to suck at communicating effectively, and I would never come between your relationship with God if you felt that my beliefs

Neither of us knew it at the time, but she would also become a personal witness to the power of God in both our lives. Each morning I'd awake and witness the living words spread out across the wall. I'd get up and record them in pen or pencil.

Throughout the day, however, for some reason the words never showed up. It was only as I awoke, early in the morning when they were visible. Week after week after week this continued. I applied deep breathing meditation to my daily routine, helping calm my mind from whatever worries threatened this newly found peace. Then came the angelic visitors. These meetings often made me second-guess my sanity. *Could Tammy be right? Was I losing my mind?* But everything flowed so smoothly, it felt so right. I was more energetic, joyful, aware, peaceful …There was so much to concern myself with, but whenever I submitted in prayer or studies, all inner turmoil vanished instantaneously. Month four …month five …winter came.

The roaches didn't like the cold. This allowed me the freedom to really concentrate on this new relationship I was developing with God. I had to unlearn so much bad information I had gathered growing up: "Don't question God…" "Man is God…" "Man is all powerful…" "You'll get rewarded once you get to heaven…" "God hates us…" A never-ending list of lies and bad theology. The opposite had proven true: God was encouraging me to ask Him questions. This was the only way I could learn the truth of who He is and who He had created me to be. He opened my eyes to how man had manipulated His Word, claiming to be God passing down this incorrect knowledge full of pride. Man was not God. But man did have a direct connection to God and was able to communicate with God unbrokenly through submission to Christ. So did woman. Only in Christ were they able to partake in this divine nature given by God's Holy Spirit. This was man's true oneness with God—in spirit, not flesh.

Growing up I had heard it preached over and over about how the promises of God and rewards of God were of old or were awaiting us in heaven. It was like God shouted to me, "Really?!!" The absurdity. But I had believed it. And why wouldn't I? My family and the church said so. But God was saying differently. I had to humble myself daily as I gave Him permission to break the bondage on my mind in order to perceive His absolutes. It wasn't hate or rage that He displayed towards me, but love. Genuine, unconditional, undeserved love. I didn't even love myself. "How could you?" I questioned. Yet, He did and began showing me through His word and actions that He always had.

In the beginning there was a plan. That plan had extended all the way down to my life and family tree.

"How couldn't I see these things before?" I asked.

"You weren't ready."

He taught me about the various stages of maturity, spiritual maturity, and how so many Christians refuse to grow up in the lessons due to being creatures of comfort, unwilling to crucify the desires of the flesh. God had offered all Christians a huge advantage when it came to doing away with old thought patterns and ways. The Holy Spirit was the actual fixer-upper. He was the one who empowered us to obey God's word. We weren't required or expected to obey on our own. That was one of the main reasons Christ had been sent to earth. To give us his spirit. Only those who are led by the spirit of God are sons of God.

"The number nineteen, Lord . . ." I asked, "...what was the meaning of that number constantly following me?"

I believed so deeply in this number having a significance in my life that in 2014 I had gotten it tattooed on my chest.

"Psalm 91."

The number nineteen had been a riddle. A mysterious message that I was finally permitted to decode. God had been present my entire life! I wanted to hide so much of what I'd done from his memory.

"But why the pain, trouble and sorrow?"

"The sins of your forefathers, those of your fleshly D.N.A."

"So, my dad and even his father had the opportunity to alter the course of their own lives and mine, but had refused. It really was a personal free choice for each of them and not just something that was inevitable?!" I became infuriated at my bloodline. But the anger was not what God wanted. He was giving me the opportunity to break the mold.

"Forgive them," He whispered to me. "What?!" I was hysterical.

"How could I?!"

"Just as I forgave you." The words sent chills up my spine. But I still needed time. He was patient with me.

"So, what about Islam?" I needed the truth.

"Stages. Experiences. Each one designed to help you grow. In order to know what is truth, you must know what is untrue. I am the Creator of all, but only the Father to some—those who accept my son Jesus."

"So, what about my aunt and cousins? What about everyone who hasn't accepted your son?"

"I have given man free will. I will not violate that. Those who reject the truth will go to hell." I shuddered at the revelation.

"What is it you want from me?" I wondered.

"An intimate relationship." God was even answering my thoughts! "But why me?"

"I desire this relationship with all my creations, but not everyone is willing."

Willing. That word resounded. This mysterious, infinite, omnipotent Creator wanted a relationship with me? A man who had murdered, stole, lied?

"How can I trust you?" I flinched at my own thoughts. Little did I know at the time how brutally open and honest I could be with Him.

"You will." He surely was confident. Scripture reveals that God knows everyone who will respond to His call for a relationship far before we are born or have any knowledge of Him. In this re-learning state, my mind was unable to grasp such wisdom. I mean, I struggled with comprehending how this was the same God of Abraham, Isaac, Jacob ...the same God of Moses, of Noah ...of Adam and Eve. Even before the earth's foundation!

"But who made you?"

"Before me no God was formed, nor will there be one after me. I, even I am the Lord and apart from me there is no Savior." No Savior? I pondered. Oh! Christ. The Savior of the world. I recalled the Scriptures: 'A Savior has been born to you; he is Christ the Lord.'

This was how God and Christ had identified themselves to me; 'Lord.' 'Savior.' Their oneness was undeniable. My head pounded from thinking so much. Where was this leading? A relationship. Okay, but what would I have to do exactly?

Mistakenly thinking that every inmate around me was undergoing the same revelations, I opened up to them about my conversations with God in search of human understanding and connection. Since I was still in segregation, I could only write notes and slide them underneath the doors of fellow gang members and associates. Why did I do that? I was laughed at and called crazy. Only a couple inmates out of dozens were actually spiritually conscious to the point of relating to my transition.

The gang life had to go if I wanted to embark committedly on this new journey.

So did relationships that were toxic. Tammy included. That was most difficult. Her andI had been a couple for two and a half years and were friends for over seven. Letting her go was painful, but keeping her close was even more painful. She wanted me to place her above my relationship with God, going as far as to state exactly that. The fear I felt when considering doing such a thing combined with the profound sense of love and admiration for God, overpowered what she demanded. Gradually, the emotional and spiritual distance chipped away at our old foundation. This had been the only woman I'd gotten on one knee to propose to. The only one I believed was worthy of my devotion. God had other plans and as I continued in faith; learning, growing and spiritually increasing in a relationship with Him, his plans became my own. Not out of obligation, but out of love and delight.

Sometime during my sixth month in seg' my second criminal appeal was denied.

My family wanted to pay my lawyers more money to re-file in the higher courts, but I couldn't stomach the idea of perpetuating the lie of Demian's false confession. I knew it wasn't right in the beginning. And with this new enlightenment of God, there was no way, I knew he would sign off. So, I had to tell my family the truth. It was terrifying, because I had fed them so many lies about being innocent. They were greatly invested in my freedom; handing out flyers to college students at Akron University, building myFacebook and YouTube pages, finding lawyers and private investigators, meeting with pastors and newspaper journalists, contacting the NAACP. But it had all been a lie, selfishly instituted for something I ached for. Freedom.

After days of intense prayer, I broke the news to them by way of phone. Their reaction wasn't anything like I was anticipating.

"That's okay Jacky. Don't worry about it," they encouraged. "What?! Did you hear what I said?" I asked, puzzled.

"It was a huge lie. All of it! I'm not innocent. I committed two murders and paid Demian to confess to help me get out."

"It's okay. We love you. Trust in God. He will bring you home."

I couldn't believe what I was hearing from them. They weren't the slightest bit upset at how I manipulated them or the court system. God's presence and power was at work.

'Trust in the Lord' I heard whispered within.

"Wow," was all I could say.

CHAPTER 5

A day after God told me about Psalm 91 being the riddle of number nineteen, He used a complete stranger to hand me a book titled *Psalm 91 God's Shield of Protection* by Peggy Joyce Ruth. My mind was blown. I was learning how God's spirit worked through people to accomplish His purposes, to answer prayers, etc. It was scary at first, I must say. After all this was God revealing himself to man. His timing was so spot-on with these encounters with others that I could only stand in amazement time after time.

In Scripture, I studied the way the Psalms are arranged and found that Psalm 91 is labeled an "orphan psalm" because it lacks superscription. There are thirty-four out of one-hundred and fifty labeled as orphans. These thirty-four are very unique and special to God. They are not labeled like all the others or given any musical notations. There's no human author claiming credit for writing them, even though King David is said to have written over half the psalms. Psalm 91 as God had shown me was a covenant psalm between himself and man. It is a bilateral psalm, representing both God and man since God first made a covenant of protection with man. In this psalm are the details of great covenant benefits for those men and women who make God their "dwelling place."

The relationship that the Lord had extended to me was a covenant one, I realized. Covenant being an agreement between us two. A contract.

Can two walk together unless they have agreed to do so? (Amos 3:3)

A couple nights before receiving this covenant book, I'd been studying Joyce Meyers, *Me And My Big Mouth*. There was a chapter within this book that broke down how to properly align oneself with God and increase your life. I recall it vividly. Joyce wrote what she did to bring about a radical change in her own life, issuing her Royal Decree. This interested me because I always viewed this woman as being highly favored by God. She went on to write about how the reader should do the suggested activity. It was around 11:00 p.m. by the time I completed penning my own Royal Decree. I stood in the middle of the cell by myself and spoke in faith the words out loud, page after page (five in total), three times before deciding that would be enough. I lay down to sleep.

That morning was the first morning I began to hear the audible voice of God and witness the writing on the wall.

I wish I could say that after agreeing to walk in Covenant relationship with the Lord things have been a breeze. That's far from the truth. But things have been worth it. The internal and external peace, the favor of God, the manifest presence of God, the incredible love and joy I feel. It continues to be worth it. But there has been a great deal of suffering in the flesh I've had to do. This is the dying to self Christ teaches all believers about. We must lose our life in order to find it. Decreasing so that God increases. Becoming less. But through this process we become more. More of who God is and who He has created us to be. And this is the process where countless Christians refuse to submit or are not taught by the church leaders. For this they suffer greater in their spiritual life and their fleshly (natural) lives. It is only through this obedience that a Christian can grow in the favor, wisdom, and stature with both God and man. (Luke 2:52).

Just hearing the word 'suffer' makes our flesh cringe. Any emotion or feeling that causes us discomfort, we seek to immediately pacify in any way we can. Some of us are taught at a early age that suffering is for those who are poor or less fortunate financially. I heard an influential preacher say that she didn't know if God allows suffering. In a nutshell, God permits suffering in order to purify us. The suffering and glory of the servant in Isaiah, Chapters 52, 53 and 54 teaches us about how God's glory can only emit from within us after suffering. Yes, it was prophesying the Messiah, but those Scriptures point to us as well. Christ suffered for our impurities, not because he was impure. He carried our sins, lived in the flesh and therefore had to suffer in the flesh, but was glorified by God.

> "I have given them the glory that you gave me, that they may be one as we are one: I in them and you in me. May they be brought to complete unity to let the world know that you sent me and have loved them even as you have loved me." (John 17: 22,23)

God's glory is his power, excellence, goodness, favor, presence; the nature and acts of God in self-manifestation, i.e., what He is and does, as exhibited in whatever way He reveals Himself. 'God made manifest' within and around us is supposed to be the Christians consuming desire in life. When John the Baptist said, "He must become greater; I must become less," he spoke for all followers of Christ. Scripture verses that I, to this day, have difficulty wrapping my mind around are the ones that speak of how Christians are to possess the fullness of God: Ephesians 3:19; Colossians 2:10; 2 Timothy 1:6. We've fallen so short of our calling and purpose. But God has a plan!

There are many teachers of God's Word in the world, but few who actually stick to the purity of the word. It's impossible to walk with the Lord or grow in Him without obeying Him. In order to obey Him we must study the Word and develop that close intimate oneness relationship with Him through submission to the Spirit. This is the only way to spiritual maturity. You can't say, "I'll take this section of Scripture, but not that one because it doesn't feel right." Living on feelings got us here in the first place.

Lost. Spiritually blind. God doesn't want only half of you, so what makes you think he'll settle with you taking only a portion of him? It's all or nothing. If you want to experience the new life on this earth that

God sent Christ to give you, you have to be willing to sacrifice. There's no greater privilege, honor and joy than to be filled to the fullness of God!! I continue to elevate in Him and I can't get enough!

I will set him securely on high because he knows my name.

If your desire is to increase in life in all areas, it first starts with humility. Pride says, 'I know it all' or 'I don't need to read this part.' Humility says, 'Lord, what is it you want me to learn from this?' Humility is submissive. Pride is defensive. Humility says I may already know this or have heard it before, but it won't hurt to hear it again.

The teaching on the many names of God have been a serious cause of confusion and spiritual stagnation in the church and individual Christian lives. Too many leaders have even blindly accepted names of God that have been totally man-made without thoroughly researching the background history of them. In doing so we've caused many to stumble and fall in their relationship with God, questioning the validity of His promises held out in His Word. If you have been someone or know someone who has helped circulate this kind of confusion, I plead that you not only continue reading these divine revelations, but that you also apply yourself to seeking this truth through personal studies and prayer. I guarantee that through applying these accurate changes to your personal and community church life, you will witness spiritual breakthrough and awakening like never before. I can guarantee this because God has shown me in my personal life. His spirit doesn't show favoritism. If you seek God, He will be found by you.

God (Hebrew name Elohim) is a general term while Lord (Hebrew YHWH; 'Yahweh') is the personal and Covenant name of God and is a perpetual testimony to His faithfulness to his promises. The name Lord/LORD emphasizes God's role as our redeemer and Covenant Lord. Christ and his disciples in the New Testament identified Christ as Lord, showing oneness with God. People have a terrible tendency to use the name Lord in disrespectful ways or they use it not knowing exactly what it is or who it is they are calling upon. In Exodus, Chapter 20, upon giving the Ten Commandments to Israel of the flesh, God was adamant about it being only one Sovereign Most High God, stating, "I am the Lord your God ...You shall have no other gods before me."

Then in Deuteronomy, Chapter 6: "The Lord our God, the Lord is one." The lower case 'g' in god's shows inferiority and relates to carved images, spirit worship and even man—anything placed before God being idolizing. In Philippians 3:19 God says that those who live to please their appetites (selfish desires) are idolizing; "their god is their stomach." 2 Peter 2:19 states that a man becomes a slave to whatever has mastered him.

In Exodus 20:7 God commands that we shall not misuse the name of the Lord our God because He will not hold anyone guiltless who does so! The name Jehovah is an incorrect spelling and pronunciation of the tetragrammaton (the four original Hebrew letters 'YHWH'). Jehovah's Witnesses was founded in 1870 in the state of PA by Charles Taze Russell. Jehovah witnesses adopted the name Jehovah in 1931 (World Almanac of Facts). Far too many believers have wrongly accepted this name as an accurate translation of Hebrew. Jews are the ones who initially began removing the name YHWH (pronounced Yahweh) from texts and stopped pronouncing it because they thought the name too holy to be uttered and feared violating Exodus 20:7; Leviticus 24:16.

When God called Moses at the burning bush in Exodus 3, He instructed him on the specific name by which He shall be remembered from generation to generation.

This gave testimony to the unchanging nature and character of God: "The Lord, the God of Your fathers ...this is my name forever, the name by which I am to be remembered from generation to generation." In Exodus 6 God told Moses, "I am the Lord. I appeared to Abraham, to Isaac and to Jacob as God Almighty, but by my name the Lord, I did not make myself known to them."

Jesus Christ continued this Covenant name: Luke 2:11; Matthew 3:3. Angels descended from heaven as witness to Christ as Lord!! (Luke 2:11).

(Note to reader: Be careful what type of bible you are reading. Not all translations are correct. To avoid confusion most of my studies and teachings have come from the King James version or Zondervan NIV Study Bible.)

If you trace the name Lord back to its original translation, you will directly connect it to YHWH. Original Hebrew name. You will not trace Lord back to Jehovah because there is no pure correlation of such letters. In fact, the word Adonai was used to assist with the spelling of Jehovah. We are called to be witnesses of the Lord, but not Jehovah Witnesses. Stop using the name Jehovah.

I also plead with and encourage all Jehovah Witnesses to test the spirits as instructed by God. I am only concerned with truth. Popularity has no place in the heart of the Christian. God never revealed himself to me by any name not in original Hebrew root: Lord. Savior. Jesus. I am firmly convinced that it is okay for a believer to study and know all the general terms of God, but God does not want us sidetracked or confused about these things which they have very much done to us. Christ says it perfectly: "Holy Father protect them by the power of your name—the name you gave me—so that they may be one as we are one. While I was with them, I protected them and kept them safe by that name you gave me." (John 17:11-12) And in Acts 4:12: "Salvation is found in no one else, for there is no other name under heaven given to men by which we must be saved." No other name!!! Speaking 'Lord and Savior, Jesus Christ' says to God that you believe that Christ is the son of God and that He is one with God as Master and Ruler. It says that you believe in Christ's death (Savior), resurrection (Lord), and power (Jesus Christ) and that you believe in your unity with the father and son through the Holy Spirit. Everything you need, are and could ever desire comes through submission to that Covenant name.

"I tell you the truth, My Father will give you whatever you ask in my name ...Ask and you will receive." (John 16:23, 24) The fulfillment of your requests will come in abundance as your heart and life align with God's Will for your life. Obedience. Once you've developed this intimate relationship with Jesus Christ, you will be enlightened by the spirit and realize it is not necessary to always say, 'Lord and Savior, Jesus Christ' in prayer or conversation with God. God knows our hearts, and as long as Christ is set apart in our hearts as Lord and Savior, conversations flow more easily. Examples, such as these will happen: "Lord, I need you to..." "Abba Father, in the name of Jesus Christ, I ask..." "Help me Jesus..." "Lord Jesus..."

Earlier, when I asked Jehovah Witnesses to test the spirits, this plea was not to them alone. Instead, it was to everyone who believes there are many paths that lead to heaven or salvation. We, as humans, should always test our beliefs. The worst thing we could do in life is to never test our faith and end up in hell because we were spiritually lazy or too prideful. Never believe in something or someone just because someone else says it's true or you think best to follow another's lead. This goes for all religions and teachings. Especially those that promise us spiritual blessings and rewards. You don't have to wait until the next life to discover the truth or power of things. God says so.

And if what and who you are following doesn't invite you to test their teachings, then that should be a sign to you of impurity and that they seek to control you more than anything. It is only through tests that we can truly grow in knowledge, wisdom, and faith. A Buddhist should test his faith. A Muslim should test his faith. A Christian should test his faith. God helps test our faith! There are false prophets and leaders to this day and will continue to be. If you open your eyes, you'll see them!

From the beginning there have been people seeking to manipulate and control the masses of people through deception and lies: "The prophets follow an evil course and use their power unjustly. Both prophet and priest are godless; even in my temple I find their wickedness, declares the Lord." (Jeremiah 23:10, 11) Yes, even so many churches today. Scriptures as these are prophetic and speak of past, present and future events. One must study and pray to understand the various applications of God's Word.

"Dear friends, do not believe every spirit, but test the spirits to see whether they are from God, because many false prophets have gone out into the world." (1 John 4:1) Muhammed claimed to be a prophet of God. And perhaps he was. But his teaching; his purpose. Did he deviate from what God had intended his mission to be?

The Bāb, born in Shiraz, Iran 1819 was a man who claimed to be sent as a messenger from God. A prophet. His mission, he claimed, was to help lead his Islamic brothers and sisters to the truth about God and Christ. He taught that man and woman were equal in the eyes of God and that both could build a personal and intimate relationship with the Creator on their own ...that every human being was individually responsible for seeking God and His truth and that the resurrection of Christ and His followers was real. This went totally against what the

Islamic religion and communities were being taught. Out of fear of losing control of their people, the elders and leaders hunted down and killed him in 1850. God continues to show His love and commitment to the Islamic faith as well as His plan of salvation for them through Christ, raising up prophets to guide them out of darkness.

The Arabs consider themselves to be descendants of Ishmael, who was Abraham's son, born of Hagar the Egyptian maid servant. Arabs are largely of the Islamic faith. Is it possible for them to have descended from Abraham? Yes. And if this is so then it makes perfect sense what God has been trying to do within their religion.

First off, Ishmael and his bloodline has been blessed by God from day one (Read Genesis 18:20). However, they are not in covenant relationship with God (Genesis 17:21) and therefore can never receive the gift of the spirit or covenant blessings unless they acknowledge the truth of Christ and become spiritually adopted (born of the spirit), just as any other race, religion or people. However, since God's plan has always been the salvation of all humankind, He raises up messengers (prophets:spokesmen of God) within the tribes or people of particular groups; men or women whose roots originate from within and uses them to speak divine messages to their people in efforts to spiritually awaken and re-direct their paths of destruction.

In the law of Moses, God commanded Israel to not set a king over them who He doesn't appoint. "He must be from among your own brothers" (Deuteronomy 17:15) I believe God uses this same law for the descendants of Ishmael which is why the Bāb was raised up from among his own brothers, being relatable and undeniably connected to them and therefore able to testify more in power as a witness to God's glory and Will for man kind. But the Bāb also deviated.

I've tested Jesus Christ and the power of his name to know that what He says is truth. There is only one Spirit of Truth and that is the Spirit of Christ. Don't buy into those who say you have to wait to get to heaven to receive blessings and rewards. These are lies from the devil! God promises to reward us openly here on earth for things such as praying, fasting and giving (Matthew 6) Of course, a reward should not be our motivation. It's a privilege and honor to pray to the Father ...to know him intimately. Those acts of praying, fasting and giving, are acts of righteousness that we, as believers in Christ, do out of joy, love and obedient faith to God. The rewards for doing them are inevitable! And because Christ teaches us that the Father's Will is done on earth as it is in heaven, I strongly believe that all earthly rewarded acts are also rewarded and given to us once we get to heaven. The fact that our citizenship is in heaven while we are even here on earth (Philippians 3:20; Ephesians 2:6) should increase our faith in this. Not to say that God doesn't reserve some things solely for heaven. The notion of "wait until heaven" as a whole is what I'm addressing. The cake is in slices enjoyable for now and later. The abundant life is for both realms—natural and spiritual. Otherwise, the resurrection of Lazarus and Christ would serve far less importance. Christ's healing power, miracles and gifts would be pointless. There would be little (if any) need for the Holy Spirit.

Once I got months into studying numerology and astrology, I was fascinated by the things I was learning. So much started making sense in my life: my character, my personality, numbers, my birth chart. I was ascertaining things that were hidden. But I hit a ceiling where I couldn't grow anymore due to the lessons and experiences being limited. God had designed me to desire more out of life. I thirsted for understanding and wisdom that could not be quenched in numerology or astrology. I was not a creature of comfort like so many others. I couldn't accept limits on my life and be okay with them ...question marks as to who and what spirit exactly was behind the numbers guiding me from my birth chart. "Spirit-guides," the books called them. Nameless, faceless, shapeless spirits helping to assist me in making right decisions. Spirits sent to protect me and my loved ones. But why? How exactly? These were questions that those books could not answer. Limits! I knew that as a human being I was created far too complex to have ghosts guiding and leading me who preferred remaining anonymous. I yearned to meet my maker. In this life. And so I did.

CHAPTER 6

When a person prays confessing their sins to God, giving their life to Christ, they immediately become spiritually adopted into the family of God. Some people can instantly feel the change, others cannot. This has a lot to do with one's sensitivity level to spiritual reality, in addition to the prayer spoken. Prayer should always be out loud to God as a newcomer. It can be at a whisper, but it should always be at a tone where your ears can hear it. The more sincere the prayer (grieving, wailing, pleading), the greater the revelations. God commands us over and over in His Word to speak out loud to Him, our mountains (obstacles), and for what we want. Because, truth is, until we learn how to calm our minds with God's help, which involves sanctification, we'll never be able to hold any fruitful conversations with God internally due to so many distractions from the many voices and thoughts bombarding us. There's so much noise that overpowers the voice of God. Even though God can easily speak and silence it all, He wants us to experience His gentleness and love on levels we've never known. This is part of His sharing with us. But even after we've given our lives over to God, there's still a re-birth process that begins and will take place for the rest of our natural lives.

Being born again is not just a play on words Christ used. It's real. It's a spiritual birth that equates the natural new birth of a baby. The natural has to go through countless stages of development: cartilage, bone, brain, organs, emotions. The same is true for the newborn Christian, except that the change has more to do with the heart (soul, mind): attitude, personality, emotions, behaviors, choices. This new transition is what makes us new creations and unveils to us the truth about who God is, who we are, our purpose in life, spiritual perception, etc. It's the process of unlearning and re- learning. God taught me ways to help accelerate this new growth. These methods are extremely vital to an individual believer. Jesus modeled and teaches us:

1. *Fasting.* Christians think they don't have to fast. It's uncommon and uncomfortable. But it's the Lord's spiritual law. There's an entire chapter, Isaiah 58, dedicated to true fasting. (When you study this chapter, don't get caught up on the things you are not required to do or cannot do while fasting, such as if you have no position at your job to help "loosen the chains of injustice.") The purpose of the chapter is to show the unchanging nature and character of God and His Will for our lives. Fasting is a part of you becoming less; you deny the flesh its natural state. Natural food is only good for your natural body and cannot sustain the spirit. Spiritual food gives life to both your natural and spiritual body because the spirit is more powerful than the natural. Don't take this out of context. All human beings need natural sustenance in life. Everything in balance and moderation. We are to avoid any and all extremes. When you fast from food that should be a time of deep prayer, studies, praise, fellowship, giving. I even like to avoid watching TV or playing games. It becomes a time of intense focus on serving God and growing in His Word and leaning into His voice.

There is always increase in some way in my life. It's a time of self-denial, self-humbling, repentance and drawing near to God. Isaiah 58 lists some rewards for fasting.

2. *Deep Prayer.* Gifts of the spirit are rarely taught anymore. Everybody wants the fruits of the spirit: love, joy, peace, etc., but

no one desires the gifts. It's like how I am with apples. I know they are a fruit and they are healthy for me. I can feel the difference in my daily routines when I include them in my diet. But I don't like doing what it takes to get them into my system; chewing and eating them. The ability to chew is my gift from God. There are nutrients in the fruit I need that can only come out by me using the gift.

When God allowed me to pass over from death to life, becoming a son with full rights, He baptized me with the Holy Spirit and the gift of tongues. 1 Corinthians: 14 details tongues and prophecy and the need for them. There's a book by Bill Johnson titled *Strengthen Yourself in the Lord* that tremendously built my faith and understanding for the gifts of the spirit.

Here's the thing—it is true that God gives us gifts through the Holy Spirit for the edifying of the church and ourselves. These gifts vary from believer to believer. But in order to help build others up we must first learn to build ourselves up in the Lord with using the gifts God gives us. Prayer reveals things. "Call to me and I will answer you and tell you great and unsearchable things you do not know." (Jeremiah 33:3) When Paul told Timothy to "fan to flame the gift of God," he was letting us know that gifts do not come in full bloom. We must use them to build them. No preacher starts off with a thousand followers. They build their congregation with God. 1 Corinthians 14:5 states that one believer can have more than one gift. We must be determined seekers of the Lord and His gifts. Prayer establishes and builds our relationship with the Father.

Prayer moves the heart and ways of God. It elevates us in every area in life. It shows submission and honor to the Lord. It strengthens faith and confirms the covenant relationship between us and Him. It's not the quantity of prayer that the Lord is interested in, but instead the quality.

    3.   *Abiding in God's Word is the only way for Him to continue abiding in you.*

Of course, everything must be in balance—prayer, fasting, studying, giving. This is the new life we are called to enjoy. God gives to us whatever we need to enjoy life and accomplish His mission of advancing the Kingdom, but there are growth stages. I can't stress this enough. It is the Lord's Word that sanctifies (cleanses) us, because it is truth. The things we unlearn are the lies and deceit and evil that we've acquired and practiced growing up. Those gaps are filled with God's truth. The truth of all things, not to be limited. It is the Holy Spirit, the Spirit of Truth, who teaches us and enables us to walk in covenant relationship with our covenant Lord.

When God was teaching me the truth about Christmas holidays and Easter and my fleshly birthday and Labor Day, I was blown away by how much true knowledge the world had been blinded from. I was mad! I debated openly in church with a pastor who had been studying and teaching God's Word for over thirty years about the solar and lunar eclipses, trying to convince him of the one-ness of all life and creation with God and His timing. Yet God humbled me, explaining to me how the truth would be rejected even by those claiming to be His most devout followers. A closed mind is a limited mind and a limited life. A closed mind is not a humble mind. We can only see God perform the impossible in our lives and in life by becoming humble. A humble mind is a teachable mind.

The Family of God

Those who are spiritually adopted into the family of God are supposed to be walking in covenant with God. Walking in covenant means obedience to the Holy Spirit's lead. This requires us to become less. The new covenant church has everything to do with the New Covenant. The old covenant is fulfilled through Christ and still has relevance. I've heard pastors teach otherwise. For us to understand the covenant, the church, the times we are in we need to look at Christ and what He accomplished by coming to earth.

There shouldn't be any doubt as to the truth of the bible extending back as far as it claims, nor should there be any doubt about the events that have taken place in Scripture simply because there's far too much physical proof supporting it. There are countless museums that you can visit to observe the reconstruction of specific instruments, tools, etc. that are mentioned in the bible. People have rebuilt Noah's Ark in exact measurements and dimensions given in the book of Genesis. One of these locations of observation is in Columbus, Ohio. To this day archeologists continue to unearth scrolls and artifacts that were mentioned in the bible. Places such as Egypt, Mount Sinai, the Red Sea are all locations on maps that people visit.

The synoptic gospels: Matthew, Mark, Luke and John—they were all personal witnesses of Jesus Christ and the Word manifesting. As they carried forward this truth; performing healings, teaching the Word, casting out demons, building God's kingdom, others became personal witnesses to the glory and power of the name Jesus Christ.

People always ask teachers of God's Word why doesn't God perform the healings and miracles that He did back in the day. They use this as an excuse to not believe in the existence of God or the truth of God's Word. But the truth is that it isn't God's fault for the seemingly endless chaos and death taking place globally. It always traces back to the church and Christians not abiding in the purity of the Word and not teaching others to do the same. The leaders. Those who distort the Word of God. The prophets who lie for profit. The preachers and teachers who were called to be great men and women of God, but who have somehow lost their way. The church's role has always been to build, guide, restore the communities and branch out into the unbelieving world with the same mission. The world is in the horrible state it's in because of the church leaders.

Churches around the globe are now being attacked on unprecedented scales by outside enemies. We've gotten away from the truth. And as long as we veer away from God, we will inevitably weaken as an individual, as a community, as a congregation, as a nation. Weakening means we remove ourselves from God's Presence, Power and Protection where we become vulnerable and defenseless against negative influences and powers.

Just study the Word. The New Testament says that all things that were written before(in the Old Testament) were written for our instruction so that we as Christians would not follow the sad examples of fleshly Israel.

Whenever Israel was attacked in the Old Testament by enemies or whenever they were defeated by an enemy, it was due to them, not God, disobeying the laws of God.

They would worship false gods, follow false prophets and leaders, rebel against those God had appointed as leaders ...the same things taking place in the churches today! "That is why so many of you are weak and sick and a number of you have fallen asleep." (1 Corinthians 11:30) Being weak and sick is not the normal state of a Christian. But Christians have been tricked into believing that being sick is the "the Lord's Will."

Remember in John 11:11 when Christ told his disciples that Lazarus had fallen asleep, but that he was going there to wake him up? Then recall Luke:22 when Jesus went to pray on the Mount of Olives and had to awaken his disciples from sleep, instructing them to pray so that they would not fall into temptation (evil). The two kinds of sleep that Christ was pointing to were:

    1.   *Physical death.* This was the death of Lazarus.

    2.   *Spiritual death.* This second death is a form of sleeping that I personally experienced in 2007 after giving my life to Christ in December of 2005. It was the same "death" and punishment Adam and Eve experienced for disobeying God in the Garden of Eden. Separation from God.

Followers of Christ have to put prayer at the top of their daily list. Prayer is personal communication between us and God and cannot be compensated by anything else. I explained the importance of prayer earlier. But this is why the church as a body has become weak and sick. A lack of prayer, seeking the Lord's Will, has caused church leaders and attendants to fall asleep, becoming spiritually out of tune and therefore open to the devil's lure. I call 2016 my re-awakening because I had fallen asleep in 2007, giving in to evil and stabbing an inmate in S.O.C.F. I was not mature enough as a Christian to know the power or importance of prayer. For this I suffered greatly for years. In Luke:22 Jesus was praying for God's strength, and for His will to be done. He asked God to remove the cup from him, but only if it was His will. It says, "An angel appeared from heaven and strengthened him." This is powerful! His prayers and ours have that power! Had he not prayed, it's evident that he would have given in to the human nature because of the powers of the flesh. He resisted temptation to the point where "his sweat became like drops of blood."

I honestly had blamed God for allowing me to fall back into temptation when I had been staying out of serious trouble for eighteen months before that stabbing.

Believe it or not, a week or so before the stabbing occurred, God sent me a dream, showing me a violent incident between two inmates where I was an onlooker. I shared this dream with one of the inmates beforehand, but I never prayed on it. I didn't know at that time how God speaks to man in riddles most times. The other inmate who was in the dream who I didn't share this revelation with was the one I ended up hurting badly. The incident unfolded in the exact same location as in my dream! This was no coincidence. It was a premonition from the Lord. Since then, I've studied and now know the importance of the dream-world.

CHAPTER 7

F leshly Israel was the original people of God. The Jews, they were the ones who Moses led out of Egypt. The name Israel, however, was initially given to Jacob upon wrestling with the angel of the Lord for blessings (Genesis 32:28). Jacob was one of the sons of Isaac and Isaac was the covenant son of Abraham promised by God. When God promised Abraham to reckon his offspring through Isaac and not Ishmael, this covenant pointed to Christ and Christians as the true seed of Abraham; the Israel of the spirit or 'spiritual Israel.' What was recorded as being carried out with Israel of the flesh in the law of Moses (first five books) foreshadowed the work of Christ and what would be carried out with Spiritual Israel. This is why God says in Exodus, Chapter 4, "Israel is my firstborn, let my son go," calling the fleshly people of Israel his firstborn son, but ultimately pointing to the coming of Christ as his true firstborn.

Throughout the book of Isaiah, the name Israel is sometimes used as referring to a nation of people as Israel and other times to an individual. The Messiah. This is prophecy.

When Christ came to earth, he identified his human (individual) body as the church/temple of God and went on to fulfill what was written about him as prophecy in the Old Testament: going to Egypt, 40 days in the desert, the transfiguration, the suffering and glory of the servant. He fulfilled the role of Israel as one man that the nation of Israel as a people was unable to do (Matthew 5:17). Equally important is the new covenant God promised to the New Testament church in Jeramiah 31. In Chapter 31, verse 31, God promised, "*The time is coming, declares the Lord, when I will make a new covenant with the house of Israel and with the house of Judah.*" Then in verse 33 he says, "*This is the covenant I will make with the House of Israel . . .*"

This new covenant we are in as Christians is only possible through Christ as Israel and Christ as the church/temple. "*I will make you to be a covenant for the people . . .*" (Isaiah 42:6). This is how each individual believer becomes a "temple" or "house" or "church" of God's spirit. The Holy Spirit. Christ is the covenant, he gives us his covenant spirit, gathering us into covenant relationship with him by the spirit. The Holy Spirit is who seals all followers and believers in Christ as Spiritual Israel (Galatians 6:16), Abraham's true offspring (Romans 9:8), as sons of God (Romans 8:13-16), inheritors of God and co-heirs with Christ (Romans 8:17), covenant people

(Galatians 4:21-31).

The Spirit adopts us, bringing us into the family of God in heaven and on earth, "on earth as it is in heaven." This is why Christ said he did not come to bring peace, but division. The division takes place between members in the same fleshy bloodline: mother and daughter, father and son. For those who are called their new family becomes the church (Luke 12:49-53). There will never be peace on earth, only peace for individual men and women who respond to God's call, in obedience. This peace is the salvation-rest of God written about in Hebrews, chapter 4. Christ is the only Prince of Peace and it is through faith in Him that believers enjoy this peace and favor in life (Luke 2:14).

"*Who then is the man that fears the Lord? He will instruct him in the way chosen for him. He will spend his days in prosperity and his descendants will inherit the land. The Lord confides in those who fear him; he makes his covenant known to them.*" (Psalm 25)

I testify to the covenant being alive and active through the Spirit who is the Lord.

Perry Stone wrote a book called, 'Deciphering End-Time Prophetic Codes.' This book helps understand prophecy. It highlights America's history as well as the history of Israel as the people of God and particular monumental events that have taken place in generations past. Perry Stone wrote of his amazement at how the timing of those events paralleled others throughout history, even down to the very month and day acknowledging God's universal rule and precise timing of activities. He emphasized April and May as being months where a lot of God's activities were clearly evident, as well as other specific months.

I began deeply studying prophecy and the covenants God made with man and found that He had even made a covenant with the moon and stars! These covenants God referred to as "fixed laws." Laws that could never be broken by the Lord. This gave me further insight into His unchanging nature.

Upon confessing my sins to the Lord and asking Christ to come into my life initially in 2005, I was brought into God's covenant family, but was not an adult heir yet, due to being irresponsible as an infant Christian. However, God's covenant timing and ordering of events in my life still manifested within and around me although I wasn't quite able to recognize spiritual reality, I noticed the month of April and May to be a time of major transition in my life year after year. I would be elevated to some sort of higher position, a better one, at whatever prison I was in. I was transferred from

S.O.C.F. to Toledo Correctional in those months in 2014. I was placed in an honor block in another year within the covenant months (nothing my behavior warranted I might add). My level was lowered from a four to a three in those same months, different year. Demians affidavit was even signed and notarized in the month of April. Huge periods of shifting for me.

In 2018 God started revealing to me this covenant timing within dreams and visions. He also revealed the Hebrew calendars, pointing out the perfect alignment of seasons and events in history and how man's life and schedule is grossly out of alignment with His. What became far more astounding is when in 2018 I seen with my own eyes

God at work in my life, transitioning me from one level to a higher one in those same covenant months after learning about them! It was both wondrous and scary. His power and presence is real. So is His faithfulness to His covenant people.

If you are someone who really desires to mature in the word, understanding and experiencing more of God's presence in ways you've only read or heard about, I'm telling you what God has taught me. God loves to teach. But we have to love to be taught.

Pray, obey, study, fast, praise. Testify when led by the Spirit. Ask God questions. Talk to Him out loud, speaking into the atmosphere. Call Him by His proper names: Lord, Abba Father, Savior, Jesus Christ. These are the personal, unchanging names of God and Christ. When He says to seek Him with all our mind, soul, heart and strength, he means just that. Nothing else is to take priority over seeking Him. Not our wife, children, friends, money, food, happiness.

Tammy had a serious problem believing that God would want us humans to place Him over our own children. I tried to lead her to the truth in Scripture, but her heart was hardened. The things and people you love in life the most and don't want to release are the same things God will remove from you in one way or another, because you are idolizing. *"Those who want to keep their life will lose it."* Telling us to give up our most precious possessions isn't God's way of being mean. It's His way of saying, *"I, the Lord, Creator of heaven and earth gave up my son for you. Who are you to deny me anything.?"* He's right. Who are we?! The very breath we take comes from Him and will some day have to return to Him.

"This is what God the Lord says—He who created the heavens and stretched them out, who spread out the earth and all that comes out of it, who gives breath to its people, and life to those who walk on it . . ." (Isaiah 42:5).

<u>What We Learn</u>

Here's the thing, a lot of teachers of God's law do not understand the importance of habitually writing down both good and bad lessons they've learned throughout their lives. They believe the only part of their life that's significant is the new life the Lord has called them to. Many of us are embarrassed by our past failures and mistakes, but God doesn't want us to be. He wants to use all things for your good and the good of others.

This is a huge part of our testimony—the things God has delivered us from.

Look at the prophets and people in Scripture. The flaws of men before walking with God and while walking with God are spoken of: Jacob was a schemer and deceiver whose name (Jacob) meant exactly that. Moses allowed his anger to get the best of him, causing him to sin against God.

David, even after entering covenant relationship with God, committed a list of sins against God by sleeping with a married woman knowing she was married and attempting to deceive the woman's husband before finally having him murdered in cold blood. What should be noteworthy to you as it is to me is the fact that none of these events were kept out of Scripture. This says a tremendous amount about the very nature of God: (1) He is truth; (2) He understands our humanness; (3) He's forgiving and gracious beyond measure; and (4) He wants us to be open and honest about our struggles and challenges.

None of those situations give us a license to sin. The Catholic church has done so much damage leading people to believe they can do whatever they want to do in life— drugs, sex, violence—as long as they confess to a priest inside a booth. They call it "confession." "Say ten hail Mary's and your sins will be forgiven," they claim. Where is this in original Scripture? People become brainwashed into believing these ridiculous claims.

The Catholic churches have come under serious charges and exposure recently because of God's patience running out. What was disturbing to me was when I learned that Catholicism is a denomination of Christianity! Why is this a problem? First off, the true body of Christ has no divisions or denominations. Christ died for this very reason. "We are all "one in Christ." (1 Corinthians 12:12-31; Galatians 3:28).

Secondly, the Catholic church has deviated from sound doctrine. NO human being can ultimately forgive another for his or her sins. Only God can and will through our acceptance of Jesus Christ by faith. Yes, we are instructed to confess our sins to one another, "So that you may be healed." (James 5:16), but we don't confess so that man can play the position of supreme authority in our lives. We confess to unburden ourselves of the guilt of sin: "*Dear children, let us not love with words of tongue, but with actions and in truth. This then is how we know we belong to the truth, and how we set our hearts at rest in his presence whenever our hearts condemn us ...if our hearts do not condemn us.*" (1 John 3:18-21)

Feelings of guilt disturb our peace. It is impossible for us to rest securely in Christ when we are troubled, worried, anxious, etc. Confessing to one another allows us to share in the fellowship of humility. We are openly acknowledging our imperfections and shortcomings. Our human-ness. Humility in Christ in this kind of prayer (confession with others) is what has the power to heal us. The Holy Spirit is the one who lives in each and every believer, and has the power to vitalize life and apply God's salvation to our lives. He enables us to obey God's commands. And He is the one who communicates God's truth to us. He is the Spirit of Truth.

Please don't get this confused. It is not always necessary to confess our sins openly to other believers. Our primary relationship needs to be with the Lord Jesus Christ. Genuine fellowship with other believers develops solely from our fellowship with Christ. Even now, as I sit in cell number 202 in Garner Correctional in Newtown, Connecticut, there aren't many believers in this block who I can strongly fellowship with. Maybe two. But that is enough.

I know that the Lord has called me to teach his Word. This privilege can be very lonely as it relates to human relationships. But I see how God was shaping and molding me from my childhood years to not be severely dependent on any other relationship than his and mine. And now, at this stage in my life, I've matured in peace with few closely connected friendships with other human beings. My connection with the Lord is so profound and powerful that I wouldn't trade it for any earthly possession or desire. I can honestly say that I love the Lord with all my heart, soul, mind and strength and I love my neighbor as myself.

How do you know when you love the Lord with all your being and your neighbor as yourself? You know by your priorities. When God is number one in your day-to-day breathing. You know it when you can pray, "Lord, your will be done for me, in me and through me today," without flinching at the idea or stammering over your words. You know it whenever you experience feelings of compassion or sadness towards an enemy you have every human right to hate. This is the heart of God, the mind of Christ that Jesus displayed when praying on the Mount of Olives asking God to remove the cup if it was His will only ...when Christ had been nailed to the wooden beams of a cross and soon after cried to the Father to forgive those who had crucified, beat, mocked, mistreated and eventually killed him.

This level of intimacy with the Lord is the most precious gift ever. Becoming less is all about sacrifice. You must give if you want to receive. But your motives must be pure. Only Christ, the Word of God, can purify our hearts. We must come to the end ofself.

CHAPTER 8

I was transferred to the Connecticut prison system from Ross Correctional in Ohio on 1-31-2017. The difference was night and day. After thirty-two years of violence, drugs, gangs, chaos and negativity (although rays of light did break through at times), God delivered me to a place where I could truly begin walking out this covenant union with Him.

There was an even more serious breaking process I soon discovered. I'd been so damaged mentally and emotionally that it took over a year just for me to mentally adjust to being in a prison system that was "peaceful." I expected Connecticut to be like Ohio's system. I was prayerful I wouldn't have to use violence to establish myself and earn my respect, but I'd become so familiar with this way of life that I couldn't fully appreciate what it was God was doing in my life for months in. I was conditioned. But with the help of the Holy Spirit, God slowly chipped away at those old patterns of behavior.

To date (1-15-2019) I've been in Connecticut two years and haven't gotten into any acts of violence or illegal activities. Two years may not sound long, but trust me when I say that from the life I formerly lived, it's long. It's the salvation of the Lord first and foremost that has kept me out of trouble, because several times my anger nearly got the best of me, or in fact did and yet I "somehow" managed to take another path in the climax of the flames. Through these tests I learned to submit to the Spirit's teaching and leading. The battlefield of the mind is a real place. Joyce Meyers' book on this study assisted me tremendously with this war. Instead of prison rebellions, in Connecticut I've led bible studies with multiple inmates in attendance and prayed over those in need. The Lord steadily increases me and prepares me for my Expected End. (Jeremiah 29:11)

I do know that there are actual innocent people in prison. But for those whose lives as once free men aligned with the eventuality of death or incarceration or the in between (wheel-chair, coma), we must accept our placement in these facilities and institutions and begin looking at them in a more godly view that can help us rise above our limitations. We must accept that at some point in our lives as free men we were out of control to the point where God deemed us unstable and unfit, our crimes leading us here in a setting that serves to assist us with regaining control over our lives through structure and order. True, prison life can be very unpredictable. But the intended structure of the day: meal times, groups, programs, recreation, are consistently arranged to give us order and to help us learn proper balance and management of our lives. Cages were not originally designed for humans, but for animals; to tame wild beasts. The invention of a small space or cell for holding a human, formed over time by man as he sought ultimate control and domination over another.

A prison cell is an unnatural environment created inside the mind of man. Being content with this state is in essence being content with existing inside the thoughts and ideas of man. But these are not God's thoughts or plans for you. God's thoughts toward you are of freedom in every aspect, prosperity, and life. However, to bring order out of disorder God will use man-made inventions to humble us, bringing us to repentance. He did it to fleshly Israel and He does it today, *"Today, if you hear his voice, do not harden your hearts."* (Hebrews Chapter 4; Psalm Chapter 95).

Renew Your Allegiance!

Whether you are in a prison, in a hospital bed, in the streets living, in a halfway house, in an abusive relationship, in a group home or in a juvenile center—it doesn't matter. Your age, placement or location has no control over what the Lord Jesus Christ can do and wants to do in your life. If you're in a religion, cult or gang and are fed up of living a life you've known deep down inside is not right for you, where you've already questioned yourself a hundred times, but could not come up with an answer as to the choices you've made or have been manipulated into making, I'm writing this to you! It is because of you that I have been called. And it is because of the love of Christ I have been chosen. That drug you are using will inevitably wear off. It's only a temporary solution, one that can over time kill you or cause you to make worse choices. I've been there. You are more valuable and precious than you know. Christ wants to show you your worth. He's standing at the door of your heart, but you must answer to let him in. He wants to heal you of your broken heart, of your pain and anger, of the un-forgiveness that has darkened the clouds above your head. He wants to free you of those bondages that have held you back from being who you were created to be. The cuffs and shackles on your mind as well as your body. He has the power. All He needs is the permission.

Your permission. Accept Jesus Christ as your Lord and Savior and allow Him to take control over your life. You've allowed drugs, violence, men, women, money to control you for so long. Why not relinquish control to who it rightfully belongs to? He won't let you down. Renew your allegiance. Pray this out loud from your heart:

"Heavenly Father, I confess my sin to you. I am separated from your presence and power due to sin. I humble myself before you today and ask that you take control of my life through your son, Jesus Christ who died on the cross so that I may be re-united with you on earth and in heaven. Change me Father into who you have created me to be. I know your ways and will are perfect. Therefore, I want to be one with you in every area of my life. Give me a new heart. Cleanse me of selfish ways. I surrender to you. Help me grow in your Word and learn to trust and obey you. I need you. Enter my life Lord, and live through me. In Jesus' name I pray. Amen."

If you prayed this from the heart, you have now become a child of God. Jesus is your brother. The Holy Spirit is your Counselor and helper who will guide you with his spirit into making better choices in life. The more you submit through prayer, studying, and obeying God's Word (the Holy Spirit will supernaturally enable and empower you to do so), the more you will increase in the presence and power of the Lord. God will heal you from the inside out. He will transform your thoughts and desires. He will open doors that no man can shut and close doors that no man can open. He will change your circumstances, creating new opportunities and friendships. All you have to do is sincerely seek him. Have faith. Pray. Fast. Study. Obey. A balanced life is a healthy life.

Remember that God is spirit and that He now lives in you. He will use other people (believers and unbelievers) to accomplish his will in your life and to answer your prayers. Other times He will have angels effect his will, but never will he leave you alone. This is a promise from God. Study the Scriptures. Start in the gospels of Matthew, Mark, Luke and John. Apply your mind and body to being still, as you study and God will open your eyes to see things hidden. Ask questions out loud at a whisper. Get in the habit of this. Be open and honest. He can take it.

Now that you have renewed your allegiance to the Lord of life, I pray that He brings healthy covenant relationships into your life that will help you mature and strengthen. I declare that all bondages be broken from your mind and body as you willingly submit to His spiritual laws. It will be a process. No genuine friendship fully blossoms overnight. You will stumble at times. But through stumbling, your understanding of the Lord's will and persistence will be strengthened. You are now an open heaven. Your thoughts, prayers, verbal words are all spoken in the temple of God before ever reaching the ears and minds of others. This is one of the reasons we are instructed to tame our tongue. Study the book of James. Spend daily time in praying and studying even if it's only a couple verses. Here is a personal word from the Lord:

> *"The Lord your God commands you this day to follow these decrees and laws; carefully observe them with all your heart and with all your soul. You have declared this day that the LORD is your God and that you will walk in his ways, that you will keep his decrees, commands, and laws and that you will obey him. And the LORD has declared this day that you are his people, his treasured possession as he promised, and that you are to keep all his commands. He has declared that he will set you in praise, fame and honor high above all the nations he had made and that you will be apeople holy to the LORD your God, as he promised."*
>
> Deuteronomy 26:16-19

Dying to Selfish Desires

> *"I tell you the truth, unless a kernel of wheat falls to the ground anddies, it remains only a single seed. But if it dies it produces many seeds. The man who loves his life will lose it, while the man who hates his life in this world will keep it for eternal life. Whoever serves me must follow me (obedience); and where I am my servant also will be. My Father will honor the one who serves me."*
>
> John 12:24, 25, 26

In the New Testament, wheat is often spoken of figuratively as representing the righteous (followers of Christ). All followers of Christ begin first and foremost as baby Christians (kernel's). The process of dying to self ("...falls to the ground and dies . . .") is what truly begins our journey as Christians going from children to adults in the Lord. God clearly tells us that we must surrender—"*Unless a kernel of wheat falls to the ground.*" This "falling" is by choice. The alternative is that it remains only a single seed.

In 2005, after I had been in the Ohio prison system for over two years, I was so miserable inside that I just wanted my life to be over. I'd gotten into a physical altercation with a rival gang member that resulted in my jaw being broken in three different places. I was placed in the medical area in October for two months with my mouth wired shut. The liquid diet was so terrible that I refused to drink most of the meals the prison-kitchen sent up to me. My weight plunged rapidly. Since I hated being a skinny kid all my life this had even more dire consequences on my psyche.

In December I was forced out of the medical area and placed in a regular segregation unit for the remainder of my recovery. Months prior, I had received my second life sentence which ran consecutive with the 30-life I was handed down in 2003. I confessed to the second crime of murder, taking a "plea deal" before being transported back to S.O.C.F.

While at S.O.C.F. I came up with a plan to get out of that particular prison because it was so awful. My invention of lies got me shipped to a protective custody unit in Toledo prison for a brief stay, which was where I underestimated an inmate, turning my back on him after having heated words, when he punched me in the jaw from the blindside while my mouth was open as I was talking to another inmate. Twenty-one years old, double-life, with a broken jaw sitting in seg. I was tapped out. The pain medication the nurses brought me assisted with the physical torment, but internally I had no fix. The psychotropic meds I was prescribed were temporarily suspended because I had a history of stacking them up. But even when taking them as prescribed, they weren't much help. The side effect were so bizarre that the meds produced odd behaviors.

As I sat alone in the cell, I had a sudden desire to write the chaplain: "*Dear chaplain, can you please bring me a bible? I don't have one. I also need you to pray for me. Thank you.*"

Even after climbing the ranks later in my bid to become a gang leader,

I always maintained respect and politeness towards staff and prison officials I considered worthy. The chaplain had never done me wrong. Plus, I was the one in need. In a matter of no time a man appeared at my cell door with a bible and a smile. Sliding it to me through the cuff-port, he asked if it would be okay for him to pray with me.

Uncomfortable, I agreed.

He spoke a nice short prayer before encouraging me to read the Word and keep faith. I was excited to get a bible. I'd never owned one before. I began searching, and as if God had been waiting on this very moment, He began speaking through His Word.

Day after day I'd awake, study and pray. I was drawn to the writing on the pages. They were powerful. Wise. Deep and rich in meaning. This was new.

It was prison tradition for inmates to bang on cell doors and yell and scream at the time the ball was dropping to bring in the New Year. As the 2005 year came to a close, God moved my heart to pray on my knees at the bunk to bring in the New Year instead of banging. I submitted, "falling to the ground" on my knees in streams of tears and sobs that flowed out from a place with no shortage of water. My heart. The Holy Spirit was at work within me. And although my life of violence and manipulation would soon continue, this was the very moment and time I was reborn. For the next eleven years of my life in prison I would face more trials, pain and fears because of my choices. Little did I know God was with me at every stage. And because of this I learned how to see in the dark. I grew.

> "...While the man who hates his life in this world will keep it for eternal life."

When I initially studied this verse, it sounded like a cruel punishment from God. Why would he make a person who hates his life keep it? I pondered. It made no sense to me especially in light of my new belief that God is merciful and good. As I grew, the Lord revealed to me that it was not a punishment, but rather a privilege for a man or woman to keep the life they hated. How so?

Well, as for me, the times I attempted suicide, but was unsuccessful, the hate I had for my life seemed to call upon more grace. Scripture teaches that God gives us more and more grace as we need it. Grace is

God's undeserved kindness, his forgiving love. Sure, there are many, many people who hate their lives with the darkest of feelings and thoughts and are successful at suicide. But Scripture also teaches that God knows far before our birth into this world who will respond to His call to a new life within the old one and who will not. I am saved by grace through faith. Period. But genuine faith is marked by obedience, not just believing in my heart. I should've been dead! If not by my own hand then by the hand of one of the many enemies I made in the life I lived.

When God saves us from our old, empty way of life the new life He has planned for us begins to exert itself into our lives as we obey the Lord's guidance. This new life involves the overwhelming power of God, at work in our hearts and minds transforming us into new creations. Re-birth. Redemption. The old things pass away (addictions, behaviors, desires) and we are brought into the divine glory of the Lord sharing as co- heirs in the blessings of God through Christ. This new life is a privilege to live and it continues for all eternity (spiritually). I've written four books before this one, none of which have ever flowed through me so effortless as this one. Those other books focused on glorifying me. I wrote of them during my time serving in the kingdom of darkness and used to wonder why I had so much difficulty getting them published. None of them were ever meant to be published! They were "practice works" to help develop my skills and talent of writing over the years.

Through death to self (as a kernel) a man or woman is able to bring forth and give life (producing many seeds). The kernel must perish as a kernel if it wants to become a plant. A caterpillar has to be re-born if it wants to become a butterfly. We must lose our life in Christ if we want a new life. This is my new life.

CHAPTER 9

I *must become less," workbook and study.*

There is work to be done here on earth! Philippians 2:12-13, "Therefore, my dear friends, as you have always obeyed—not only in my presence, but now much more in my absence—continue to *work out your salvation* with fear and trembling, for it is God who works in you to will and to act according to his good purpose."

Now that you have accepted Jesus Christ as your personal Lord and Savior, there's some things you will have to do to assist with spiritually maturing in God's Word. There are people who have been Christians for thirty, forty and fifty years, but who have matured very little throughout their time. For this reason, they don't get to enjoy the full blessings and promises of God, the power of God, nor are they equipped with the wisdom that only God can give to carry out their service and mission while here on earth. They are not convinced of their purpose and service, because God will not reveal it to anyone who does not commit to seeking and obeying him. Some are convinced that a powerless life is a normal state for Christians. Whenever God does answer their prayers, they're not motivated or stirred in spirit to seek greater things from Him.

God doesn't want us being content with erratically answered prayers. He seeks to draw us near. The more we learn about who God is the more we grow in His wisdom, favor and the knowledge of our purpose(s) here on earth. The more we mature in these ways the more passionate we'll be about obeying Him. Stop being spiritually lazy! The TV shows, sports, games, fruitless books and conversations can all wait. Put the Lord first.

Whenever I finish studying a Joyce Meyer, T.D. Jakes, Bill Johnson book or any spiritual book that can help my growth I say to God, "Lord I finished the work that you gave me to do. Please show me what's next." It may take two weeks, four days or a month to study a book, simply because I don't just read it. I speak to the Lord out loud, asking for wisdom if I don't comprehend specific chapters or sentences. I mark-up books like a mad man—underlining, circling, highlighting and making notes for myself and others I may pass it along to. I memorize whatever I am moved to memorize and if there's an activity included in the book, I do it. This is the discipline and passion the Lord expects and admires from his covenant people. Christians.

Books such as from the authors I've listed (not to exclude the countless other authors I've studied from) tremendously help to build and even accelerate a believer's growth in the Word. Many of the Lord's humble followers have stupendous firsthand knowledge and experience walking with the Lord. You can discover, through studying their books, what to do in certain situations as well as what not to do. As I mentioned earlier, Joyce Meyers' *Me and My Big Mouth* book dramatically changed my life!!! Ask the Lord to lead you to a book in the bible or a book from a Christian author that will aid your maturity in Him.

So what if you don't like the way someone preaches on TV or what others say about them. It's not about that, it's about getting all God has for you in every area: wisdom, blessings, new life, identity. Even if you've been walking with God for many years, if you desire a life of increase this is how you get it. I'm living proof. And so are a sea of others! I'm not the first person to be saved by God, to witness His power and miracles or to write a book giving testimony of Him and I won't be the last.

The command to "work out your salvation" is not a reference to earn your salvation by works. Salvation is a gift from God in response to putting faith in Jesus Christ. However, as I previously wrote, genuine faith is marked by obedience (James 2:14-26). The work that a Christian is instructed and assisted in performing through the empowerment of the Holy Spirit who lives within each and every believer, is work that builds us up to becoming wise evolved Christians (spiritual adults) in contrast to remaining an infant (kernel). Through this evolution we manifest more and more of the fruits of the spirit in our daily lives. This is an ongoing process and cannot be substituted for anything else. The Lord rewards us for our sacrifice and obedience.

I encourage you to complete the following study. Take your time. Make checkmarks next to Scripture verses you want to study deeper. Speak with God about what you are learning. Pray for understanding.

I was once looking around in my cell block unit for someone who I could share with what I was learning. Before I could begin to zero in on a possible believer, the Lord whispered, "Share with me." There will be periods in your life (especially when God is doing a serious work in your heart such as when you first give your life to Christ) where you feel alone, having no one to connect with or relate to on a human level. Even when there are many believers in your life never forget or underestimate the power of conversation with the Lord. It will serve the same, if not better, purpose as if you are sharing with another person. You'll be enlightened by the revelations God will send you. You'll feel liberated, comforted, joyful ...It's the spirit at work within us who produces supernatural joy, who comforts us, opens our minds to understand and free us!

Communicate with God: "*Lord I need . . .*" "*Father help me to . . .*" "*Jesus please . . .*"

For the Lord is the spirit and where the spirit of the Lord is, there is freedom.

Workbook Section

(1)   How old were you when you gave your life to the Lord? (Write down month, day and year, if you remember). You may have been a young child when you first gave your life to God, but don't remember much other than what family or friends told you. It's important to renew your allegiance to the Lord when you are older. It's like a marriage. Some people marry young and don't recall the moment vividly, so they remarry later in life. It's necessary to turn your life over to God as a conscious (aware) being. In faith, speak the salvation prayer or pray from the heart using the salvation prayer as a guide.

(2)   Psalm 91 is a covenant psalm between God and man. God promises that those who dwell (abide, live) in Him (through study, prayer, obedience) will rest in His presence. This rest is peace of mind, spirit and body (total peace) that only Christ gives. He is 'Prince of Peace.' By abiding in Christ and Him abiding in you your life begins to gradually (inwardly and outwardly; internal and external) display this salvation-rest. Study Hebrews, Chapter 4, which details this promise of rest for the people of God. Are you in need of this divine rest? Explain how you want your life to be. Are you anxious, fearful, depressed? Explain.

(3)   The Lord promises that if you open wide your mouth He will fill it. Write out a list of five things you would like the Lord to fulfill for you. Sign and date it. As God answers your prayers date each request the day he responds. This is the beginning of your prayer journal. Please keep in mind that some answers may take weeks or years to be manifested, but keep faith because the Lord is faithful. He may be preparing you for the blessing. As you keep steady in this relationship, trusting and obeying, He will amaze you by fulfilling the desires of your heart (Psalm 37:4). Remember the meaning of the name you are calling upon. Lord. He is faithful to His promises. "*For no matter how many promises God has made, they are yes in Christ*" (2 Corinthians 1:20) Write down prayer requests as you need to.

(4)   What have you learned so far from reading/studying

this book? Can you relate to any part of it? If so, which one(s)?

(5)   Are you willing to give up your way of living so that Christ can live through you? Explain what parts of your day you can sacrifice to pray and study the bible.

(6)   You are a child of God. The Lord says, "*Can a mother forget the baby at her breast and have no compassion on the child she has borne? Though she may forget, I will not forget you. See I have engraved you on the palms of my hands.*" (Isaiah 49: 15-16) What does this mean to you?

(7)   The Lord wants to restore your life in every way. In order for Him to refresh your life you must be willing to repent (turn away from sin and turn to him in faith). The Holy Spirit will supernaturally enable you to obey when you are sincere about repenting. Pray out loud from the heart, asking God to cleanse your heart and help you submit to Him.

(8)   If you're reading this in a prison cell you must understand it was the Lord who caused you to be placed in captivity. Even if you didn't commit a crime to be incarcerated, God still desires a relationship with you! He has a purpose and plan for your life. Even a man who is in prison who is not guilty of a crime is not truly "not guilty" until he accepts Jesus Christ as Lord and Savior. The Lord's forgiveness is what ultimately matters. Study the following verses: Jeremiah 29:11-14; Deuteronomy 28:41; Deuteronomy 30:16.

(9)   God's will is that you become holy. Becoming holy means at times you will suffer hardships in life. You must endure hardships as discipline. "*No discipline seems pleasant at the time but painful. Later on, however, it produces a harvest of righteousness and peace for those who have been trained by it.*" (Hebrews 12:11) Are you learning from your hardships?

Chapter 10

Freedom in Christ

Jesus Christ being the Savior of the world means just that. Those who accept the only begotten Son of God are not only delivered from their sins, but also the consequences of them as well.

What does this mean exactly?

When people believe in Christ as their Savior, God declares them to be Not Guilty. He cancels the guilt of their sin and credits righteousness to them. That is why Scripture teaches that there is no condemnation for those who are in Christ Jesus. "No condemnation" means no guilt. Christ died to pay the penalty for our sin and lived a perfectly righteous life that can in turn be imputed to us.

"...*salvation from our enemies and from the hand of all who hate us ...to rescue us from the hand of our enemies and to enable us to serve him without fear and in holiness and righteousness before him all our days.*" (Luke 1:71, 74, 75)

To serve the Lord in holiness without fear and in righteousness is to participate in the covenant benefits that come with submitting to the Lord. "Without fear" equals covenant benefit. "In righteousness" equals covenant benefit. "To serve" equals covenant benefit. "Salvation from enemies" equals covenant benefit. "Rescue" equals covenant benefit. "Enablement" equals covenant benefit.

Christ is the mediator of the new covenant. Deliverance from consequences, enablement to obey; these benefits come only through Him. By accepting and submitting

This freedom in Christ that a Christian is to share in involves mind (from bondage), body (from bondage) and spirit (from defilement).

It is complete freedom to be who the Lord created you to be: A child of God, in service to God, walking in peace and unity with God.

When the Lord first began sending me dreams and night visions of Him setting me free from captivity (prison) I was so excited. I was anticipating it would happen in a matter of days or weeks. The dreams were so clear and aligned perfectly with Scripture. Time after time I would pack up my property, handing out my valuables to inmates in the Connecticut prison system as a blessing to them, informing them that I was on my way home only to be utterly devastated when that expected day would come and go. My circumstances remained unchanged. I would be furious with God over and over again, not understanding. He would guide me to certain Scriptures elaborating on His will, but because I was trying to control Him and His timing, my heart was at times hardened. I wanted things when I wanted them. Over time he broke me of this selfishness. I submitted to his wisdom and was joyfully learning to trust that he has my best in mind. The promises never changed—even in my willful disobedient moments. As I repented and pushed forward in faith, I grew in His wisdom and power.

God has revealed to me my purpose in life and daily prepares me for my future, walking and serving with Him. I am a New Creation. The old has gone. It has been a growth process and it will be the same for you.

"Write down the revelations and make it plain on tablets so that a herald may run with it. For the revelation awaits an appointed time, it speaks of the end and will not prove false. Though it may linger, wait for it; it will certainly come and will not delay." (Habakkuk 2:2, 3)

Learn from my mistakes if you want to avoid unnecessary pain and tears. When the Lord tells you something or promises you something, it will come to pass. Wait for it! Write it down. Pray on it. Keep it to yourself until he tells you otherwise. There's a time to keep the Lord's revelation secret and there's a time to reveal them to others.

Now is my "appointed time" of revealing. Two years ago, was not the case.

Submission to Rulers and Authorities

I was transferred from Ross Correctional prison in Ohio to MacDougall-Walker prison in Connecticut on January 31, 2017, the same day of the birthday of the famous baseball player Jackie Robinson. After going through assessment at Walker intake and being issued a Connecticut prison number, I was then relocated to Cheshire institution and soon after placed in cell number 42 (Jackie Robinson's baseball jersey number) after phasing through reception. At the time I did not know how God spoke to man through his circumstances. I was witnessing the truth of Him being ever-present.

I had a tough time adjusting to this new environment because my mind and body had been programmed to rough atmospheres. Over the last two years of being in the Ohio prison system I recognized the shift my heart was taking. A lot of my old behaviors and attitudes had become unattractive to me. But I kept exhibiting these negative mindsets and actions out of fear of becoming a victim if I let my guard down. Yet I found whenever I would initiate fistfights with other inmates my heart was so far drawn from the altercation that I'd end up losing. I knew a change was occurring deeper than the surface. I had mastered being an aggressor and inflicting harm and bodily injury to others over the years. This shift forced me to step back on more than one occasion and analyze where this was headed.

Needless to say, breaking free of this kind of mental bondage was not easy. It required me to be open and vulnerable, trusting in God to protect me. I resisted, oftentaking matters into my own hands, seeking to produce results I desired, but never once did the situations get physical.

Connecticut's prison elements were so different from what I knew. Inmates were walking around in shower and house shoes (slippers) on a daily basis. They would sleep with their cell doors unlocked. They showered without having a friend or army wait outside the shower on guard for them to finish. Everyone associated with everyone.

Officers were mostly respectful and kind. There wasn't any tension in the air. Fights weren't popin' off in cells, staff weren't placing hits on inmates. Where was I?!

Inmates seen the distinguished mannerisms in me. They watched. But it wasn't the type of observance like in Ohio when inmates watched. Whenever an Ohio prisoner studied you, it was more than likely because he was plotting to rob or attack. I was programmed to notice others without giving away that I noticed. But there wasn't any need to address my observers because the threat energy was never present. 'So why watch?' I pondered. It was unusual. I soon discovered that guys just wanted to talk and be friends.

'What?!!' I couldn't believe it. I searched the eyes, handshake and words of each individual who approached me looking for their ulterior motive. Even the staff were cool and relaxed. Whenever they asked questions about who I was or commented on my"country accent" I'd respond in few words and keep it moving. I sought to isolate myself, but God would push me out into the open. I found it very frustrating when the prison would be repeatedly locked down over and over again for small matters. The inmates would obediently march to their cells without protest.

I wasn't used to this; to complying with this level of oppression, at times becoming the voice for the people. But none of the inmates seemed to care or were aware of their oppressive state. I stuck out like a sore thumb each time I mentioned concern. For nearly a year this rebellious mentality persisted. God was trying to show me how to submit to His will through submission to instituted authority.

"Submit yourselves for the Lord's sake to every authority instituted among men." (Romans 13; 1 Peter 2:13)

I twisted and turned in the hands of God, attempting to free myself from discomfort. I prayed, "Your will be done," but the fire of being salted through His will had me begging for mercy. I was a mess. Years of unrighteous ways and fostered pride being broken like eggshells as I lay breathlessly in the palm of the Lord.

'Would it all be worth it?' I asked myself time and time again.

Then there was the love I had come to feel for the Lord. I was head over heels in love with this mighty God. To deny Him anything, just the thought of denying Him broke my heart. He had been denied too much by us humans. This I knew. The voice of the enemy was loud, "God doesn't care about you! Look at what you're going through!!"

My own thoughts followed, "Why am I doing this? I should give up. What if I don'tmake it?!"

The Word and prayer were the only things that proved effective against periods of doubt. The more I studied the more I retained Scripture passages in my mind and would be able to recall the necessary ones to combat fear, anxiety and worry. At times, however, the promises of God felt so enormous that I had difficulty believing them:

"Offspring of Abraham." "Co-heirs in Christ." "With you." "Restore you . . ." The Lord understood my struggle. No longer was it a fight between me and man.

It had now fully existed in the spiritual realm. I wrestled with the Lord over my faith.

<u>Repentance to Bring Blessing</u>

> "*Return, O Israel, to the Lord your God. Your sins have been your downfall. Take words with you and return to the Lord. Say to Him:forgive all our sins and receive us graciously, that we may offer the fruit of our lips ...who is wise? He will realize these things. Who is discerning? He will understand them. The ways of the LORD are right; the righteous walk in them, but the rebellious stumble in them.*" Hosea 14:1, 2, 9

Our sins have been our downfall. Individually as well as a nation and world of people. We obsess over materials, popularity, technology, gossip, but few of us obsess over God and truth.

"What is truth?" Pilate asked in response to Christ saying he came into the world to testify to the truth.

Truth is the Lord our God is one. God is truth. God is love, it's not just something He does. Truth is that the Lord God did in fact send Jesus Christ to a world in need. This truth clearly shows God being love, in action to redeem us and reconcile us to Himself. Our sins had left us separated from Him! If it had not been for the Lord's grace (undeserved love) in sending Christ, we as humans would've destroyed ourselves or been wiped out by God from this earth just as those who were wiped out in the flood in Noah's day.

From the beginning the covenants God made with Noah, Abraham, Moses and all others were all made and fulfilled in and through Christ. Sending Jesus Christ had always been God's plan once Adam and Eve disobeyed God. The Lord knew man was weak and powerless on his own to overcome the evil one, flee from temptation, purify himself and walk in humble obedience to God. Only by abiding in the Lord's power through the Holy Spirit are we now able to receive and share in those covenant blessings.

Who is the Spirit? The Lord

Who is the Lord? Christ and God. They are one. Inseparable. Truth is the Lord has already forgiven you for your sins, but awaits you to call unto Him in acknowledgement and confession of your evil, accepting Jesus Christ into your heart and life. Christ does not have to come to earth and die again for your salvation. It's already prepared at a table for you, but unless you "open wide your mouth" you will remain in a spiritually dead state on earth and afterwards an eternal fire.

"Return," urges the Lord. Repent: forsake sin and turn to God in faith through His Son. If you've gotten off the path of salvation, Return! If you're seeking the path of salvation "turn" this way! Repent. The words you are to take with you in repentance are to be sincere to the Lord. From the heart. The Lord promises: *"I will answer him and care for him."*

The Lord's care is not like man's or woman's. There's no love to be found on earth that can compare or be equated to that of the Lord's. God uses earthly metaphors of "husband and wife," "son and father," but once you've actually felt and witnessed His love in your personal life, metaphors as these cannot define or explain this love. No words can. God loves you. Yes, you!! That's truth.

CHAPTER 11

F or me, time never flew by in prison as some inmates claim it did for them.

Perhaps because I stayed in segregation units so much throughout my years of incarceration. But I have to say that I felt every moment of being locked away. Since prison moves at a far slower pace than being free does, this allowed me to really take in things that were transpiring around the world on the news. The uprising of school and church shootings troubled my soul most. These violent attacks on innocent children moved me to tears more than once. I was like a lot of people initially, blaming God until He opened my eyes to the truth of what was actually happening:

Micah 2:9 *"You take away my blessing from their children forever."*

This is what the Sovereign Lord declares to all those who are in position to lead and teach the truth about God, but who have gone their own way with lies and deception. The cowardly, lazy spiritual leaders who have shrunk back from their purpose to the people. Each and every teacher of the word of God is supposed to be a covenant for the people. Their role is to love the Lord and others, worship the

Lord in all they do, draw close to God, learning His truth (becoming Christ-like), teach the church to do the same and call unbelievers to repentance in Christ, gathering them to the body of Christ (church).

This is the light, life and freedom Christ taught. This calling is from darkness to light. In this light, life is full ...abundant. The power of God and presence of God is manifested through His Holy Spirit. There is no sickness, disease, weaknesses or lack in a body that possesses the fullness of God. Individually or collectively. Why not?

Because God is not sick or weak or diseased. The covenant people help bring others into the Lord's covenant to share in the blessings and protection of the Lord. The lord's salvation frees us from all bondage to be who we were created to be, to live and walk out our purpose.

The violence on children and churches happens because the blessing and presence of the Lord is not with them! God clearly states why these things happen.

> "*Hear this, you leaders of the house of Jacob, you rulers of the house of Israel (covenant men and women), who despise justice and distort all that is right; who build Zion with bloodshed, and Jerusalem with wickedness. Her leaders judge for a bribe, her priest teach for a price, and her prophets tell fortunes for money.*
> *Yet they lean upon the Lord and say, 'Is not the Lord among us? No disaster will come upon us.' Therefore, because of you (false leaders, false messengers of God), Zion will be plowed like a field, Jerusalem will become a heap of rubble, the temple hill a mound overgrown with thickets.*" (Micah 3:9-12)

Man has removed the teachings of God out of schools and has built churches that promote racial divide. America's power and influence was originally built on biblical laws. Bloodshed, yes. But God's spiritual laws also. This is why there are Scripture verses and acclamations to God written and engraved on the Liberty Bell in Philadelphia, the Washington Monument, in the White House, in the Library of Congress, in the original Constitution and Bill of Rights. This land and people made oaths to the Lord God to walk as free people in covenant with him. The Lord upheld his end of the covenant, prospering America beyond measure. But we broke faith, turning to our own ways and devices in pride and arrogance. Those who had been anointed to lead and keep this country in alignment with the Lord began using their freedom in Christ as a cover-up for wickedness. Money and control became the focal point of those anointed. The sheep, led astray, accepted this new direction and message abandoning God's moral laws that brought life and completion to the human soul.

This confusion of God's way of life was passed down to generation after generation, creating a weaker and weaker state of human existence with each succeeding generation. The churches encouraged beer and wine as they skimmed through Scripture, taking out what appealed to their flesh while starving their spirit. The devil smiled. God continued raising up leader after leader as promised to David, Abraham and Moses and fulfilled in Christ, each with the same purpose and mission: "*bring my salvation to the end of the earth.*"

As I watched news hour after news hour of the direction and shape the world had taken on the surface, it appeared to me the devil had won, the schools and churches being the claimed trophy for his evil kingdom. I felt ashamed to be in prison. I was no better than a mass shooter. We had both done criminal acts of violence resulting in death, mine just on a lower heinous level. I knew, however, in my heart that I was not the same man I'd been at eighteen. But the stigma of prison still terribly bothered me.

Even when inmates did change their life, submitting to spiritual law, other inmates and staff who'd known them from their former ways weren't truly respectful or convinced of their shift, making it more difficult for them to live out a completely changed life as an inmate. The Ohio prison system destroyed guys like this. So, I would pray. I'd pray for those inmates who were struggling to survive or change ...For those who had made mistakes as a free man or woman, but who were wishing for a better life.

I prayed for the churches, America, for the world to be shown mercy by God ...for the many schools and families who'd been affected by gun violence. Instead of judging the president, I would pray for him—for the Lord's will to be done in and through him no matter what. I'd go to God in tears, pleading His will be done and that He keep patience with our evil.

The scary thing about walking in darkness is that you cannot see where you are going or heading. This light I was given opened my eyes wider than I could ever imagine. The tiniest acts of violence, even the cries of a newborn baby, deeply touched the heart and emotions of God. His pain became my own. We wept together.

"*Jacky, I need you.*"

His words and voice resonated throughout my entire being as I exited a church service one Sunday evening in Cheshire Correctional. This Maker and Ruler of heaven and earth needed me?!! I was humbled to my knees.

"*What is man that you are mindful of him, the Son of man that you care for him?*" King David questioned. I too could only wonder as the Lord promised to prepare me for His purposes. The penning of this book being one of them.

"*There is no peace, says the Lord, for the wicked.*"

The Lord is calling out to you today, at this very moment, as you read this. He's knocking. Pleading. With you. With us. As an individual. As a nation and world of people. Repent. Return to the covenant commitments.

> "*Come to me, all you who are weary and burdened and I will give you rest. Take my yoke upon you and learn from me, for I am gentle and humble in heart, and you will find rest for your souls. For my yoke is easy and my burden is light.*" (Matthew 11:28-30)

We must renew our schools' allegiance to the covenant of the Lord. Our churches. Our communities. Our land. Ourselves. If not, bloodshed under the curse will only increase. Captivity will increase. Mental illness and sickness will increase. Only for those who revere the name of the Lord and submit in obedience to the Lord will receive beauty for ashes. We must become less. Look around at the world where you are and ask yourself, 'How can I help?' The Lord will prepare you.

All He needs is a willing vessel. Get ready to be amazed!

"At the renewal of all things"…
Dear Parkland, Newtown…

Over the past few years, I've seen very powerful moments on the news with both teachers and students in staggering numbers walking out of schools in protest against gun violence as well as pay for educators. This has taken place globally and has been very impactful on the education system. I've witnessed famous people step into this wave with words of encouragement for those marching, but not once have I seen one of the Lord's anointed step up on the platform to raise the spiritual consciousness of the minds and hearts of so many affected souls. This too, I prayed in eagerness for.

Thousands of children had taken to the streets in 2018 speaking out in boldness to political leaders worldwide. I could see the ambition in their young eyes yet also the fear and confusion; 'why did this keep happening?' Shooting after shooting. Death after death. The panic to be heard. The need for change—any that would result in safer schools! The speeches each child gave. The tears and pain. The loss of so many close friends and family members. I understood. I understood their dire need to speak out. The role of those who were appointed to prevent tragedies as these abandoned. Such intense anger and rage in their innocent faces, unaware that their complaints had been misdirected.

Only a true Savior could save. Only he or she who had been anointed could represent this Savior to a world in need. A Christ-figure. The mayor, governor, president were not the ones at fault. Nor were they the ones who could implement permanent change. What was needed then is what is needed now.

The welfare of all nations of people on this globe and those authorities instituted over them (judges, governors, kings and queens, presidents) depends first and foremost on those anointed by God to make intercession (prayer on behalf of the people and offices). It is their submission to and reliance on the covenant Lord that actually directs the path of history.

"The Lord is Lord of heaven, earth and sea. He gives breath to all people walking on earth and establishes and uproots all kingdoms of the earth. He governs the affairs of man and all His purposes shall be fulfilled."

It is no longer by force or might that a man is to rise to power in a political or royal office, but by the Lord's spirit. Man keeps fighting wars here on earth that Christ has already defeated in the spiritual and heavenly realms (*"We wrestle not against flesh and blood..."* Ephesians 6:12).

Had I never sought to elevate in life and remained fighting "wars" on a physical level, I would not be writing this book and I would not be where I am today in my relationship with the Creator. I would still be trying to protect myself and pave my own way to no avail. I would still be living in fear and anxiety with no peace. We don't walk in victory, because we have not surrendered our will to the Lord's.

"For the battle is not yours but God's."

When Christ said his kingdom was not of this earth, He was talking about a kingdom that man could obtain through force, flesh and pride. The kingdom of God is spiritual and is let down on earth invisibly in different ages or periods of time the Lord has set. This is how Christ remains forever (John 12:34). It is through the hearts and lives of his people who help expand the territory of His spiritual kingdom on earth that He remains. The visual parts of the kingdom can be seen through the spheres of influence the Lord's people have on earth. Wherever they go to teach and expand the kingdom becomes evident. It's in the hearts and changed lives of others who share in this expansion.

"Your kingdom come, Your will be done, on earth as it is in heaven." The kingdom comes and the Lord's will is done through believers. Remember Christ said, *"The kingdom of God is within you."* What is needed at this moment is for the men and women of God to gather together in the greatest fast, prayer and praise movement of all time. We must seek the counsel of the Lord making written petitions for what is needed on this earth: Righteous leaders of God in political positions; power and influence to be restored to the churches; bondages to be broken off the minds and bodies of all of God's people; purity in spreading the Word of Truth; an

opening of the hearts and minds of allpeople; the tearing down of all evil, division and corruption within the sacred body of Christ; renewal of the covenant in churches, schools and nations; restoration of peace and prosperity of the land; divine guidance and protection. The Lord is faithful and will answer!

Groups of two and three believers are good, but if you can gather with ten, twenty or a hundred people, then you are rewarded with more responsibility. If you've recently given your life to the Lord, you are now a believer and your voice will be heard on high. Come together. If you are in prison, come together! If you are free, come together!!

This is faith expressing itself in action. Write out your petitions.

"Dear Lord, we are gathered here today in honor of your name..."

Write in detail what is needed for your community, environment, body (individually and collectively). It can be one page or ten. Detail it. Date it. Sign it. Allpeople. Pray over it all three days (If you can only fast for twelve hours, that's fine.

Break the twelve hours into three sets of four.) Deny your flesh.

Day one (or the first four hours) include singing and praising—new songs to the Lord. You can make them up! Study the Word, pray for His spirit to lead you to Scriptures.

Day two (or the second four hours) pray more intensely, study, deny your flesh.

Day three (or the third four hours, equaling twelve hours) praise, rejoice, study.

You will feel the power and presence of the Lord in and around you. His approval and delight. Even if you are alone, such as I was when I first learned how to fast, you can still use this model and will reap the benefits. Denying your flesh is to deny fleshly desires: entertainment, food, pleasures. Anything that excites your flesh. Deny yourself as much as you can, giving more focus on the Lord. You will grow stronger in the Lord each time you fast. I fast whenever I am led by the spirit. Drink water when you fast.

Sometimes I drink fruit juice, but refrain from anything I'd have to chew, even candy. Me and a Christian brother went on a forty day and night liquid fast abstaining from any and all solid foods. We used milk, water, protein powder-shakes and fruit juices to sustain us. We were inspired by a book by Lou Engle titled, *The Jesus Fast*. It was a very powerful period and did wonders for and over the land we were in.

> *"Some men came and told Jehoshaphat, 'A vast army is coming against you from Edom, from the other side of the sea . . .' Alarmed, Jehoshaphat resolved to inquire of the LORD, and he proclaimed a fast for all Judah. The people of Judah came together to seek help from the LORD; indeed, they came from every town in Judah to seek him. Then Jehoshaphat stood up in the assembly ...and said: 'O Lord, God of our fathers, are you not the God who is in heaven? You rule over all the kingdoms of the nations. Power and might are in your hand, and no one can withstand you. O our God did you not drive out the inhabitants of this land before your people Israel and give it forever to the descendants of your friend Abraham? They have lived in it and have built a sanctuary for your name, saying, 'If calamity comes upon us, whether the sword of judgment, or plague or famine, we will stand in your presence before this temple that bears your name and will cry out to you in our distress and you will hear us and save us . . .' We have no power to face this vast army that is attacking us. We do not know what to do, but our eyes are upon you."* (2 Chronicles 20:2-12)

It then says that,

> *"All the men of Judah, with their wives and children and little ones stood there before the Lord. Then the spirit of the Lord came ...Do not be afraid or discouraged because of this vast army. For the battle is not yours, but God's ...You will not have to fight this battle...'*

What had the people of Jerusalem and Judah done to receive the Word, power and presence of the Lord? They became less. They denied their flesh and their own devices and ideas under the spiritual leadership of one who was anointed. Jehoshaphat.

> *"Jehoshaphat bowed with his face to the ground, and all the people of Judah and Jerusalem fell down (death to self) in worship to the Lord. Then some of the Levites from the Komatiites and Korahites stood up and praised the Lord, the God of Israel, with very loud voices ...Early in the morning they left for the desert of Tekoa."*

It does not say they ended their fast or praises the next day after receiving wordfrom the Lord, instead:

> *"As they set out, Jehoshaphat stood and said, 'Listen to me Juda and people of Jerusalem! Have faith in the Lord your God and you will be upheld; have faith in his prophets and you will be successful.' After consulting the people, Jehoshaphat appointed men to sing to the Lord and to praise Him for His splendor of His holiness as they went out at the head of the army, saying: 'Give thanks to the Lord, for his love endures forever.'"*

Since Jesus Christ lives in you through His Holy Spirit, you have become the "temple of the Lord," your body possessing the presence and glory of God. This temple"bears His name." The Lord is enthroned in each and every believer, but you must become less so that He becomes greater in your life. Work out your salvation.

In the Old Testament God chose David and his dynasty to be his royal representatives on earth. The Lord chose Jerusalem (the city of David) as his earthly throne. Jerusalem (Zion) became the earthly capital (and symbol) of the kingdom of God. In this palace (the temple), God's people could meet with him to bring their prayers, praises and to see the Lord's power and glory. And from that earthly palace theLord brought salvation, dispensed blessings and judged the nations. The Lord's goodwill and faithfulness toward His people was symbolized by His pledged presence among them at this temple in Jerusalem, the "city of the Great King."

Chapter 12

*C*hrist in you, the hope of glory."
As a living, breathing temple of the Lord our God, everything God has created you for, blessed you with and wants to do for, through and with you works itself out and into your life as you submit to the spirit's lead in obedience. The promise from the Lord to always be with you is fulfilled by the sending of the Holy Spirit. The Spirit of Truth.

"He will be with you. He lives with you and will be in you."

This is the Lord's pledged presence! This is how an inmate can be in a cell by himself experiencing the power and presence of the Lord, praying and praising the Lord, meeting with the Lord without ever leaving out to find a chapel. Individually, we are the church. The Lord gathers us to himself with other believers in churches and chapels built on earth for fellowship, unity and family. The more we gather together in true worship, self-denial, and purity of the Word, the stronger the

Lord's presence and power enters our lives, communities and world. This is the righteous order that is needed.

One that will be fulfilled.

> *"Don't you know that you yourselves are God's temple and that God's spirit lives in you? If anyone destroys God's temple, God will destroy him; for God's temple is sacred and you are that temple."* (1 Corinthians)

> *"Do you not know that your body is a temple of the Holy Spirit, who is in you, whom you have received from God? You are not your own; you were brought at a price. Therefore, honor God with your body."* (1 Corinthians 6:18-20)

..........*

As for this section, I was unsure if I should write what follows. However, I was watching the Nightly News at 6:30, and a story came on about churches increasing "hired gun carriers" to guard and "protect" the congregations during services.

Apparently, over the past ten years this has become more common in different states.

I became so angry with the spiritual blindness of Christians that I broke out in tears as I prayed. Some things began to make sense. It was not my own anger, but the Lord's I was sensing in every fiber of my being. He spoke, saying not to be discouraged, that the victory was ours in the end. The end being the end of the wicked system of things ...the end of the age controlled by satanic domination when God would permanently renew and restore all things through the spiritual offspring of Abraham in Christ. Christians. But this had not always been the Lord's focus. He had options.

Two years ago, the Lord revealed to me in a vision that he was strongly considering allowing a foreign enemy to destroy America with missiles. The vision was very clear and compelling. In it I saw the devastation in the streets from the attack.

Cars were blown up, bridges were destroyed, countless lives lost with very few survivors. In this vision, God revealed that the world's obsession with technology had blinded the hearts of the people. Everyone was serving these systems and gadgets. Idolizing. We had bowed down to them in reverence.

America launched missiles in counterattack, but I was only shown the impact the war had on this country. There was smoke and ash all over the streets as I stood in a group of three others discussing what was transpiring. God revealed to me that it was Russia who He intended to use to bring about this chaos.

I sought the Lord in prayer—deep, emotional prayer. I did not know at the time why his thoughts were so hostile toward us, although I did know we as a nation were severely broken and corrupt. I prayed, pleading for his mercy and permitted the Holy Spirit to intercede for me because I ultimately wanted the Lord's will. I didn't know exactly what to pray for; judgment or grace. That night God spoke to me in a dream promising he'd cancel his judgment of destruction. He showed me a huge X on the moon over my head made by his finger signifying his covenant word. Cancelled. I thanked Him.

The Lord has a message to all those men and women within his body who are condoning and perpetuating this false way of serving Him. He knows the fear you have in your hearts, but this fear is not found in his body—it is an ungodly fear. A fear that arises only by the church and believers conforming to the pattern of this world. A fear that enters through unbelief and impure doctrine. You will be destroyed by that same gun you bear. Any armor that is not of the Lord's will be stripped from you and used against you. Return.

God's protection is in his covenant relationship with you as individual Christians and as a collective body. This is a promise made from the Old Testament to the New.

> "*I am the gate; whoever enters through Me will be saved. He will come in and go out and find pasture.*"
> (Translation: The one way to salvation. Inside there is safety and one is able to go out and find pasture, i.e., the supply of all needs).
> (John 10:9)

> "*We know that anyone born of God does not continue to sin; the one who was born of God (Christ) keeps him safe and the evil one cannot harm him. We know that we are children of God and that the whole world is under the control of the evil one (Satan). We know also that the Son of God has come and has given us understanding so that we may know him who is true. And we are in him who is true—even in his Son Jesus Christ. He is the true God and eternal life. Dear children, keep yourselves from idols.*" (1 John 5:18-21)

When Christians break from sound doctrine, we are no longer on the narrow road that is life. All roads do not lead to salvation. This is how the devil enters the doors and homes of believers. We are then led astray, conforming to the wicked system and kingdom. God's moral laws are sacrificed and we become, once again, enslaved by sin.

We then sway others, weakening their faith. The Spirit of Truth cannot guide us into truth because we are no longer aligned with Him. Instead of overcoming the world as a Christian is instructed to do by truth, we go over to the side of the world that is spiritually blinded. We become vulnerable to all sorts of attacks—mind, spirit, body, no longer under the divine protection and guidance of the Lord. We've abandoned the covenant.

This is what happens when we read from various translations of the Word of God without first researching to see if it is an accurate translation. Or when we study from only the New Testament believing that the Old Testament no longer has application.

This is what happens when we stop praying daily, regularly, or when we stop challenging our faith ...when we don't test the spirits of those men and women around us who we are learning from. This is what leads to spiritual blindness, confusion, fear, lack of faith, vulnerability, powerlessness, problems and condemnation. Satan is aware, so why aren't we?

It is of the utmost importance to stick to sound teaching because the Spirit testifies of the truth. The Holy Spirit reveals to our spirit the truth of who God is and life. A bible that has been stripped of even a small fraction of truth limits the Holy Spirit's presence and power in our life. It limits our ability to believe in God's fullness, His power, in you and for you. Paul was in constant battle with men coming against the church in his day who taught from unsound doctrine.

It is impossible to keep in the commands of God when one is out of touch with the truth of God. A believer who believes God is evil or unjust our double-minded will convince himself that it's okay for him to be the same. Because of our lack of study we fill in the blanks on our own painting pictures of who we want or believe the Lord should be. I had a female friend who was like this. She convinced herself that God was who she had created in her mind. We paint Him out to be our personal genie and then blame Him whenever our wishes do not come true. But he has promised:

"I, the Lord, do not change."

When out of alignment with truth, it's our perception of Him that shifts. Our obedience to His truth enables us to walk in victory without fear. Obedience is the key to blessings, living out our purpose, elevating in the Lord, complete salvation, power, overcoming the world…

"God is light; in him there is no darkness at all. If we claim to have fellowship with him yet walk in the darkness (evil, false ways, ways of this world) we lie and do not live by the truth." (1 John" 1:5, 6)

"We know that we have come to know him if we obey his commands. The man who says, 'I know him' but does not do what he commands is a liar and the truth is not in him. But if anyone obeys his word, God's love is truly made complete in him. This is how we know we are in him: whoever claims to live in him must live as Jesus did."
(1 John 2:3-6)

There's a reason why we do not know the exact time and date of

Jesus Christ's birth as a baby into this world. Scripture is very clear about the timing of his death, however:

"*At the sixth hour ...until the ninth hour . . .*" (Mark 15:33; Luke 23:44)

And his resurrection:

"*Early on the first day of the week . . .*" (John 20:1; Luke 24:1; Matthew 28:1;Mark 16:2)

This is significant for a number of reasons. I remember praying and begging theLord to let me go home before my 33rd birthday in 2017. I had plans to spend it with my dad, stepmother and fiancé, Tammy. I had stopped celebrating my birthdays in prison years prior, seeing them more as negative reminders of another year incarcerated.

As a little boy, birthdays weren't anything to celebrate wherever I resided. I wasn't surrounded with love or people who cared about me to surprise me with a cake or gift; therefore, as an adult those annual days never truly held any influence over me.

Letting go was easy. And although I was hopeful the Lord would respond by setting mefree in 2017 before June arrived the pain of still sitting in a cell on that date wasn't unbearable. However, I did need answers. Answers only the Lord could provide.

I believed the Scriptures—that the Lord was Sovereign, that He determined the times and dates of all things ...the moments of all people's birth and location of their upbringing. So why wouldn't He honor 6-17-2017 in a way that only He could? Was I not special to Him? I quickly realized my self-pity in my questioning. Instead, I took itto Him in prayer.

"What do you honor, Lord, if not my birthday? How will I know what times and holidays are special to you so I can honor them with you?"

For the next year he walked me through His covenant timing—holy days not holidays that had been designed by man. Dates that were sacred, unchangeable, precious to the Lord and now to me. Christ's fleshly birthday ("earth day") is not revealed because it is of the flesh. The Lord does not honor the flesh. The resurrectionof Christ by the power of the Holy Spirit is given supremacy because (1) God is spirit. (2) Believers share in the Spirit and resurrection of Christ. (3) The resurrection is all about the completion of sanctification or salvation (being glorified). (4) The resurrection timing marks a new age or period of time. New life for believers. New season of life in nature.

Fleshly Israel was given the religious calendar upon deliverance from Egypt that began with Passover, unleavened bread and first fruits that Christ fulfilled.

"The Lord said to Moses and Aaron in Egypt, 'this month (April) is to be for you, the first month, the first month of your year.'" (Exodus 12:1, 2)

Joshua, who succeeded Moses, "crossed over" the Jordan River, taking all Israel into the long-awaited promised land in the first covenant month of harvest (April on the Gregorian calendar). Christ was crucified on Friday after eating the Passover meal on Thursday, fulfilling the law and giving this festival its new meaning: Lord's supper.

Christ also promised that whoever would hear his words and believe (faith in action) would possess eternal life and would not be condemned; *"He has crossed over from death to life."* (John 5:24)

It's important to study Jewish/Hebrew culture and the times of Scripture writing. The Jews sometimes counted parts of days as whole days—twelve hours equaling a day. Twelve hours for the sun to rule the sky, twelve hours for the moon to rule the sky. The three days of Christ being dead includes part of Friday afternoon, all of Saturday (Sabbath), and Sunday, being the resurrection ("first day of the week"), Jesus' body being placed in the tomb before 6:00 p.m. Friday night when the Sabbath began and all work ceased.

The institution of this religious calendar that Christ fulfills, remains as the covenant timing for God's people and the Lord's judgment against the nations. As Christians we walk in the daily and seasonal blessings of the Lord whereas unbelievers walk under the daily and seasonal curses of God. The Lord does not honor Christmas, Thanksgiving, 4th of July, fleshly births, Valentine's Day, Mother's Day, Father's Day, black history month, President's Day, Halloween, June-teenth, or the New Year inaugurated by the hands of man. He doesn't smile at them nor appreciate what man has done to hide the true meaning of his holy days such as Easter.

Man has led us to believe that Easter is about cute bunny rabbits, colorful eggs and candy. We dress up on Sunday in expensive clothes and make our way to church on a day we've blindly claimed to be a

Sabbath. Truth is every day becomes a Sabbath (sacred, holy) for the man or woman in Christ. This is the holiness God calls all believers to where our entire lives—every aspect—becomes sacred. This is the salvation-rest (a life of rest) Hebrews Chapter 4 teaches about.

America does not honor any of the three covenant holy days out of the year.

Neither do most Christians. The holidays America does honor are pagan (non-believer) holidays, none of which are holy. When I say honor, I am speaking about esteeming, revering these holy days in the Lord. Acknowledging even. The early Christians did so and even before Christ came and fulfilled them, Israel of the flesh knew them to be the Lord's covenant timing with man: *"The harvest is past, the summer has ended and we are not saved."* (Jeremiah 8:20)

April 1st is a divinely fixed date in time on the Gregorian calendar (the calendar America and most parts of the world use). On the Hebrew calendar the Passover was always observed on Nisan (Abib) 14. This being a fixed date. Before Christ's death he explained the new covenant:

> *"While they were eating, Jesus took bread, gave thanks and broke it and gave it to his disciples, saying, 'Take it, this is my body.' Then he took the cup, gave thanks and offered it to them, and they all drank from it. 'This is my blood of the covenant, which is poured out for many.'"*

The cup representing the blood of Jesus, which in turn represents His poured out life (his death). (Mark 14:22-24)

It was on the evening before his death that Jesus observed his last Passover meal and afterward instituted the Lord's Evening Meal. According to Scripture when Judas left the meal at the command of Christ (*"what you are about to do, do quickly"*) *"it wasnight"* (John 13:30).

Since the 24-hour period of a day of the Jewish calendar ran from evening of one day to evening of the next day, the Lord's evening meal was celebrated within the 24- hour period of his death on Nisan 14, 33 C.E. On the Gregorian calendar this 24-hour day fell on Thursday-Friday, March 31st – April 1st, 33 C.E. Christ's command to his followers for us to continue carrying on the Lord's Supper (*"This is my body given for you; do this in remembrance of me."* Luke 22:19) has both spiritual and physical involvement.

Christians are no longer under law, but grace. We are not required to observe the law as an attempted means of salvation or sanctification. The Spirit fulfills the law in us as we partner with Him to work out our salvation (obedience to the Spirit's lead). The law requires. Grace enables. The command to "do this in remembrance of me" instructs us to continue (physically and spiritually) passing forth and passing down the testimony we've inherited to our children, succeeding generations and to new believers.

This proclaiming of believers divine deliverance from the bondage to sin and its consequences through Christ's atoning work on the cross is what we have been commanded to "remember" when we come together, especially in the New Season of the first covenant month. Just as the Passover was a constant reminder of and proclamation of God's redemption of Israel form bondage in Egypt, so the keeping of this command by believers would serve the same purpose.

> *"You are to observe this ceremony in this month ...on this day tell your son, 'I do this because of what the Lord did for me when I came out of Egypt.' This observance will be for you like a sign on your hand and a reminder on your forehead that the law of the Lord is to be on your lips ...You must keep this ordinance at the appointed time year after year . . .' "* (Exodus 13:5, 8, 9, 10)

> *"Fix these words of mine in your hearts and minds; tie them as symbols on your hands and bind them on your foreheads. Teach them to your children, talking about them when you sit at home, and when you walk along the road, when you lie down and when you get up ...so that your days and the days of your children may be many . . ."* (Deuteronomy 11:18, 19, 21)

It's the testimony of what the Lord has done from generations past and in our lives that connects us to the promises of the Lord. This is why adhering to sound doctrine is vital. Our new life, as children of God, is alive in the Word of God! This is spiritual adoption. April 1st will always be the first day of the new life and season of God's covenant people ...the beginning of our new year, no matter what day of the week it falls on (fixed date). We must let go of the empty traditions of man and hold onto the commands of God. This is a huge part of renewing allegiance and renewing our covenant commitments to the Lord.

The next covenant day and month comes exactly fifty days counting from April 1st. May 20th, Pentecost (Harvest; Feast of weeks). Exodus, Chapters 19-24 set forth the Siniatic covenant through Moses for all Israel. Even after the renewals in Exodus 34, Deuteronomy and Joshua, the spirit of the covenant remained fixed. Every aspect of it pointing to Christ fulfilling it in us believers; Spiritual Israel, the offspring of Abraham through faith—not flesh. Hebrews Chapter 12 confirms us of this inheritance as spiritually adopted sons and daughters of the living God:

> "*You have not come to a mountain that can be touched and that is burning with fire ...but you have come to Mount Zion, to the heavenly Jerusalem, the city of the living God ...to Jesus the mediator of the new covenant* . . ." (Hebrews 12:18, 22, 24)

Pentecost for Christians is the time where the Lord shows himself in a special way as the blesser and keeper of his covenant. It is the day where the redeemed of the Lord share in the separation of the wicked and righteous ...where the end of the age ends and the new age begins ...it's the bodily resurrection of the spiritual sons of God and the return of exile for all those who have repented of their sins in captivity.

Other believers share in the restored harvest and blessings of the redeemed.

When the Holy Spirit came at Pentecost in Acts 2, look at everything that transpired:

      (1) They were given great spiritual gifts (tongues,

prophesying, powers to heal).

(2) There was a clear "separation" between the true followers of Christ and the teachers of the law of Moses (Pharisees, Sadducees).

(3) They began to live a "new life" in the power of Christ.

(4) They were "raised up" above their enemies sharing in the glory of God through Christ.

(5) A new age entered and the spreading of the gospel grew like wildfire throughout the earth, which included gentiles and all peoples.

Although April 1st is the beginning of the New Year for all believers in Christ, April 1st will forever remain the day and time of Christ's sacrifice for the forgiveness of sins. "For as in Adam all die, so in Christ all will be made alive. But each in his own turn: Christ, the first fruits (April 1st, Nisan/Abib 14); then when he comes, those who belong to him (certain first fruits, those redeemed—May 20th, Pentecost). Then the end will come (of the age)."

Only the redeemed take part in the first resurrection from the earth which is both physical and spiritual. The second raising up (resurrection) is the one where all other believers partake in. This one is spiritual only.

The third covenant day and month is September 22nd.

"*Celebrate the Feast of Ingathering at the end of the year, when you gather in your crops from the field.*" (Exodus 23:16)

As Christians we are not required to celebrate these days in the sense of how unbelievers celebrate Christmas or the 4th of July. We instead align our lives in accordance with them, enjoying each and every moment of every day with the Lord and His blessings while greatly looking forward to His annually seasonal miracles. The Spirit fulfills all these things in us. In other words, God doesn't expect or require us to make plans to be in a specific place during these covenant times outside of where the Spirit leads us. As a believer, we are not our own! We belong to Christ. Where the Lord wants us He will take us as we submit in obedience to His lead. The trouble comes whenwe resist His will in our lives.

September 22nd is the exact day in 2016 when I received the Psalm 91 book, *God's Shield of Protection* through a total stranger. I had just finished showering. The officer escorted me back to the cell in Ross Correctional segregation unit. After removing the handcuffs, he closed and locked the cuff port. I was alone. Walking overto the bunk bed I proceeded to dry myself as I marveled at the book in my hand. I paused, feeling myself mesmerized by the cover. As I peered up and out the huge cell- window facing the interior side of the prison, I noticed dense clouds and smoke advancing towards me from over the tall trees just outside the fence on a hill area.

It was around 4:00 p.m. as the day sky immediately started to darken. I'd never seen anything like it. Lightening shot out from the clouds, hitting the ground in rapid bolts in a stepping motion with several seconds in between each appearance. My heart sped up. There was a loud siren. The guard announced a yard shutdown over the loudspeaker. As the clouds drew closer and the lightening got closer I became so terrified that I crawled onto the mattress on the bottom bunk praying for protection.

The sudden storm made its way over top the building I was in, a bolt of lightening tapping the cell-window without cracking it. I couldn't believe it. Neither did I understand what had happened at the time. For a year or so after I'd honestly thought the devil had made an attempt on my life like never before! The Lord revealed it was not Satan, but Him, His descent and presence like how He had came to Israel in the desert. September 22nd. The final covenant day for the people of God.

> *"On the morning of the third day there was thunder and lightning, with a thick cloud over the mountain, and a very loud trumpet blast. Everyone in the camp trembled."* (Exodus 19:16)

Dear children keep yourselves from idols.

Distinguishing True Prophets From False

As given through Moses form the Lord God there are three basic principles for establishing the truthfulness of one of God's prophets:

(1) The true prophet would speak in the Lord's name;

(2) *The things foretold would come to pass* (Deuteronomy 18:20-22);

(3) *His prophesying must* promote true worship being in harmony with God's revealed Word and commandments. (Deuteronomy 13:1-4)

(4)

This last requirement was of the highest importance. Anything the Lord promises or speaks will always be in alignment with His Word (Scripture). The true prophet of God was an advocate of righteousness and his message focused primarily on moral standards and their application. He expressed the Lord's mind on matters. (Isaiah 1:10-20; Micah 6:1-2)

It is not necessary to wait years or generations to see whether or not the prophet was true or false by fulfillment of a prediction. If his message contradicted God's revealed will and standards (in Scripture) he was false. Christ instructs all believers to test a man or woman who claims to speak in his name or perform signs in his name "by the fruit he bears."

"Watch out for false prophets. They come to you in sheep's clothing, but inwardly they are ferocious wolves. By their fruit you will recognize them ...likewise, every good tree bears good fruit, and a bad tree bears bad fruit. A good tree cannot bear bad fruit, and a bad tree cannot bear good fruit ...thus, by their fruit you will recognize them." (Matthew 7:15, 16, 17, 18, 20)

"But there were also false prophets among the people, just as there will be false teachers among you." (2 Peter 2:1)

A true prophet of the Lord never foretold simply to satisfy human curiosity. His predictions related to God's will, purpose, standards, or judgment. (Kings 11:29-39; Isaiah 7:3-9).

Often the future events foretold were the consequence of existing conditions; as the people sowed, so they would reap. The false prophets lulled the people and their leaders with soothing assurances, that despite their unrighteous course, God was still with them to protect and prosper them. (Jeremiah 23:16-20; 28:1-4)

They imitated the true prophets, employing symbolic language and actions.

While some were outright frauds, many were evidently prophets who became delinquent or apostate. Some were women, false prophetesses. (Ezekiel 13:17-23 compare Revelation 2:20).

In these misguided states a spirit of uncleanness replaced God's spirit. Under the old law all such false prophets were to be put to death! (Deuteronomy 13:5). Under the New Covenant, the Lord promises to punish all such people.

Prophet: "One through whom divine will and purposes are made known." A true prophet of God is no ordinary announcer, but a spokesman for God, men and women of God with inspired messages. A prophet stands in the intimate circle of God and God reveals His confidential matters to them. The Greek pro.phe'tes literally means "A speaker out, before, or in front of" thus describes a proclaimer, one who makes known messages attributed to a divine source. This includes prediction of the future. However, the fundamental meaning of the word is not that of prediction. The Lord's prophets, both men and women, exist on earth today standing between God in Christ Jesus and the people just as Moses did. Christ is the mediator of the New Covenant and those who are chosen for the heavenly calling while on earth (Hebrews 3:1) become under-priests (teachers, messengers, prophets) of Christ, our great High Priest.

"*For the lips of a priest ought to preserve knowledge, and from his mouth men should seek instruction—because he is the messenger of the Lord Almighty.*" (Malachi 2:7)

At Mount Horeb the people requested that Moses take the message from God and deliver it to them (Exodus 20:19). The people were gathered as Christians are gathered into the church (congregation). The Lord agreed that a mediator was good.

Christ remains forever through the hearts and lives of his people. We must become less.

Me and My Dad on a Visit in 2016

ABOUT THE AUTHOR

Jacky has been writing books since 2007 while in prison but has only recently followed through with publishing due to the goodness of God's blessing upon his life. Incarcerated at the age of 18 for two murders, he has grown through education and spiritual enlightenment and is on a mission to restore power to the heavenly realm through spreading the truth of the gospel. Jacky is in the process of writing another book and enjoys designing businesses, working out and cooking to pass time in prison. His faith to be released from prison is set firmly in his lord and savior.

Me in Connecticut prison (Cheshire).
Photo taken in 2020.

Milton Keynes UK
Ingram Content Group UK Ltd.
UKHW050656041224
3395UKWH00050B/670

9 781637 511466